The Art of College Admission

A Step-By-Step Guide to Crafting an Unforgettable Application and Avoiding the 11 Mistakes College Admissions Officers Say Lead to Rejections

Noah Craig

Contents

Introduction

Getting accepted into college is quite a thrill. The application process, on the other hand, can be long, bureaucratic, and tiresome. It involves research, forms, interviews, and tension while waiting for a final response. Things can go several ways. You might get the response you're looking for or an underwhelming response that contains words such as "unfortunately," "we regret to inform you...," and "we wish you the best of luck...." Getting that rejection letter is rough obviously, but there are very positive ways to think about it. Lessons can be learned. Maybe that college wasn't right for you, you have different qualifications or passions than what they're looking for, or you may have made some fundamental mistakes in your application. The goal here is to improve your chances of standing out on your application and finding the right place for you. Also, to determine which skills and experiences you'll want to dig into while still in high school and how to avoid mistakes while preparing your submission.

When I sat down to write this book, I wanted to create a valuable guide for not just the college application process but for the time leading up to it and what happens afterward. There truly is an art to it all. It doesn't begin when you start filling out the forms and writing the essays. It kicks off when you're a freshman in high school, and it isn't confined to the school walls.

Throughout my career, I've had the pleasure of counseling students and their families as they applied and paid for their college education. This process isn't always taught at school, and often the chosen approach is improvising; just figure it out as you go. Trying and failing can be an effective way of learning, but for this scenario, I believe that being informed and prepared is the way to go, making minimal mistakes.

So... what do students want guidance on? Well, according to my research, pretty much everything. Different people struggle in various areas. So I set out to make a reasonably all-encompassing guide to it all without being overwhelming or unnecessarily long-winded. The stress and indecision that come with the application are enough; no need to add to that. As I said, there's an art to it all. Art to the actual application, sure, but also to building your college list, making plans after acceptance, and even when it comes to the bill. I'm hoping to make you feel a bit more comfortable with all of it. More prepared, more confident. So take a deep breath and proceed.

The Egg, the Coffee, and the Carrot

The whole process is challenging, and you'll come out a different person at the end. That could be good, bad, or both. It just depends on how you deal with it. The challenges can mold you or prove that you are unyielding.

Change can come in three distinct ways: you can be an egg, a coffee bean, or a carrot. All of them have to go into boiling water to become something else. The egg that goes in is feeble and fragile. But, as it spends time in the boiling water, it becomes something else: a harder, stronger version of what it once was.

When you pour hot water into coffee grounds, the major change doesn't happen in the coffee grounds themselves but in the surrounding water. The coffee leaves a powerful mark. I wouldn't recommend drinking boiling water, but coffee is my life's blood.

A raw carrot is hard and strong. You could chop or grate it and serve it just like that on a salad. If you boil it though (or bake, I suppose), the carrot ends up soft and fragile. The exact process that made the egg tough, and that matched with the coffee beans to create a precious drink, makes the carrot into something more vulnerable than it was.

There's nothing special about boiling water alone: These different results come from the things put into it. Think of the process of applying to college in the same way. You, more than anyone, will choose how you'll go through this undertaking. Are you going to be the egg that goes through a profound internal change and emerges stronger? Are you going to be the coffee bean that, through its particular qualities, can influence its surroundings? Or are you the carrot, which emerges from the toughness of the process softer than what it once was? There truly is no one correct answer.

An Overview

I'd like you to use this book the way you want to. Reading it cover to cover isn't the only way to go about it. Feel free to use the table of contents to find the information you need. Jump around, feel it out, and fold a few page corners. There's information about picking your electives and your classes, doing extracurricular school or community activities, testing, writing essays, financial aid, and so on.

I want to mention, though, that there's a subject that frequently is not given the attention it deserves, creating your college list. It's best if you don't rush while choosing which schools to apply to. The most famous and prestigious ones may not be ideal for you, and there are a lot of other aspects to consider besides the academic merits of the school. Think about distance, location, weather, class sizes, and, of course, cost. You need a balanced list of colleges you dream of attending, the ones you have a good chance of being accepted to, and the more affordable ones.

While the information you choose to include about yourself is vital, the way you present it will say a lot about you. There are many do's and don'ts to follow; jump to Chapter 4 if you're curious. And remember, the application process doesn't end when you click 'Submit.'

Chapter 4 is also good to reference if you're concerned about the interview. It's vital that you're well prepared, even when it comes to how you're dressed.

And then comes the essay, the bane of existence for so many during this period. But it doesn't have to be. Priority number one: don't plagiarize; just don't do it. I realize it's easy to do by accident too, but there are ways to avoid that. Even if you aren't caught immediately, know there's always a chance you could be found out after you've been admitted or even after your graduation. It can have serious consequences.

When the party is over, then comes the check. Financial aid can come in the form of a scholarship or fellowship, but you can also get Federal Student Aid or support from a private organization. Applying for financial aid can also be tricky; we'll streamline it.

When all is said and done, there's always a chance that you're not accepted into any colleges you applied to or possibly only to ones you've realized you can't afford.

Obviously, that can be frustrating, disappointing, and disheartening. But, remember, you still have options. All is not lost.

When you think of going to college, what comes to mind for many is the 'traditional' path of high school, then straight into college, possibly a year off beforehand. But many roads lead to college, and you may want to jump to Chapter 9 if you're on one of those 'alternative' roads: international and transfer students, homeschoolers, athletes, and veterans. Each of these cases calls for a different approach and has particular requirements.

As I said, use this book as you need it. How one enters their college years will look different in some small and some major ways from student to student. The journey is individually yours, and I'd like this book to be the same.

"Every artist was first an amateur."
-Ralph Waldo Emerson

1

The Building Blocks—Freshman Through Junior Year

Moving from high school (or wherever you may be right now) to getting a college degree can be confusing and overwhelming. There's a lot to do in order to secure your place at the right school, organize your time, and pay for your education, all while studying hard to maintain good grades. All of this becomes easier the sooner you start preparing.

While it's never too early to start thinking about your college application, the ideal time would be during your freshman year. At this point, you can begin to organize your class schedule, pursue extracurricular activities, visit university campuses, and even organize your social life with a focus on your future. If you are already in your senior year, don't fret, I have some thoughts for you too.

Extracurricular Activities

Colleges aren't just looking for people who can give the correct answer on a test and write an eloquent essay. They want to know if the person they're evaluating is a participating member of their community in one way or another. How you choose to spend your time speaks volumes. Your level of engagement can signal what kind of ally you will be for the school and the other students.

Not everything can be taught in a classroom. A student with a variety of extracurricular activities will have a broad skill set and generally be more aware of their strengths and weaknesses. These activities, together with your college essay, speak to who you are and what you'll bring to the table.

Freshman year is a great time to start picking out and building on your extracurricular activities. This is generally the time when you have more free time on your hands. Plus, you'll find there are plenty of things you thought you might be interested in that turn out to be something you may even hate or vice versa. The coronavirus has taken a toll on volunteering; along with everything else. It hasn't stopped, but it has changed a lot. Now, so much can be done through a computer with tools like Zoom, allowing students to offer volunteer services to people worldwide and in many different ways.

Still, you should be careful not to overload yourself to the point that you're distracted from the over-arching goal. Taking on dozens of extracurricular activities just to add them to your resume is a mistake. It's much more effective to choose fewer total activities that you have the time (and the passion) to commit to. Maintaining balance is essential, and it's a habit that will be useful once you're in college and beyond.

It's wise, if possible, to choose your extracurriculars based on what you do well and believe in. For example, there's no reason to add 'cellist' to your resume if you don't like classical music. Although a cello is sometimes used in other genres, you see my point. Neither should you try to play volleyball if you don't at least enjoy the sport, only for the sake of adding it to your application.

Also, you can ask yourself if that activity is relevant to your intended major, but don't overthink it. Maybe you love playing the cello and are great at volleyball but think that these skills wouldn't make much of a difference if you're applying to law school. Think again. In this case, you may want to try your hand with debate or public speaking as well, but don't abandon your passions. Again, balance is key here. Find harmony with what you love to do in combination with what is sure to have the most pull towards what you are trying to achieve. Great things can come from something you enjoy and do only mildly well or things you didn't even think you'd like. Give it time and dedication, and you may find something unique and gratifying about a bunch of stuff you usually wouldn't consider. Your interests will likely evolve over time, as will your values.

I see so many students making the mistake of thinking that what they enjoy couldn't possibly be considered an extracurricular that a reputable college would respect. The possibilities really are endless. They range from volunteering and participating in various clubs to video games, beekeeping, glassblowing, jobs, internships, caring for sick family members, or babysitting. You name it, there's usually a way to turn it into an activity you can include on your application.

Keep in mind that colleges will evaluate the quality of your extracurricular activities rather than the quantity. How long were you involved? What sort of impact did you have? It's okay to jump around while trying to find something you enjoy, but you want to show that you can commit to something long enough to make a mark.

You shouldn't feel like you must simultaneously be involved in everything you plan to explore. And remember that some things only require your involvement once per week, month, or even year. So work hard, but don't forget to play hard too.

Ninth Grade

While there's always room for error and learning from mistakes, most colleges will prefer students with a consistent track record throughout high school. If you start investing in yourself freshman year, your chances of acceptance improve.

The courses you take in high school will not only be listed on your transcript, but they'll also likely help you learn a few things about yourself including how you approach stressful situations and challenges and what you want to pursue. You'll have to take the required core classes to graduate, but you'll get to play with electives. Use these to explore and find out what you're interested in. Don't overload yourself, especially this early. Instead, take on what you firmly believe you can handle with poise. As you build your confidence, you might want to consider enrolling in honors courses. This will improve your chances of standing out later on. I recommend starting with honors courses and moving on to AP classes if you feel comfortable, even taking up to three in your senior year. Just remember, you'd rather have an A in an honors course than a C in an AP course. You want to show that you can push yourself but are aware and respectful of your own limits. These courses are more demanding than your regular classes, not just in terms of the difficulty of the subject matter but also likely more demanding of your time.

Electives are a great way to discover your passions and what you excel at. Of course, that could be something different than what you plan to study at college, but that isn't a bad thing. It's okay if you change your mind about your intended major. It's also okay if your electives do nothing to change your mind about the path you're on; they still have value. No worries, it's all part of the process.

When in doubt (and even when you're not), ask for the help of your teachers, school advisors, and guidance counselors to pick the courses that are right for you and hopefully will make you stand out on a college application. If you think you already know what college major or what career you'd like to pursue, talk with your counselor, and they'll be able to show you which classes are available to you that are geared toward your goals. Most colleges require students to have studied the core subjects, and generally high schools don't consider these optional anyway. Keep in mind that these will vary slightly from state to state:

- English: four years
- social studies (history, civics, geography, economics, etc.): three years
- mathematics: three years
- science: three years
- foreign language: aim for at least 3 years if not 4

If at all possible, you'll want to develop a good relationship with your guidance counselor. They'll likely have hundreds of students they're assigned to, and time is precious, so remember to be patient and always come prepared when meeting with them. In addition to getting good advice, the ultimate goal would be to show passion and commitment, making you stand out in the counselor's mind.

All high school students look forward to summer; you should certainly use this time to relax and have fun. Still, if you want to make a serious commitment to a nice, shiny college application, you'll want to use some of that time to land a job, whether it's paid or volunteer work. However, being well traveled is not a bad thing either, so that cross-country trip is by no means time wasted. You may also want to start your college research and begin prepping for the PSAT or PreACT. There are plenty of fun options that involve continuing education as well. Harvard offers a free online Introduction to Computer Science course. You can learn programming using Python through the Massachusetts Institute of Technology. I enjoyed The Science of Happiness which is offered through UC Berkely. You could easily find the summer reading lists for your current top college choices as well. Use your time wisely but do not underestimate the importance of resting and leisure.

Tenth Grade

If you're starting here, I'd recommend also at least skimming the Ninth Grade section as well.

Ah, sophomore year. Still so much time and so much ground to cover. You're getting more comfortable with the high school curriculum. If you haven't done so yet, it may be time to select a mentor, someone to guide you through high school and into college. This could be a teacher, a school counselor, a current student or alumnus of a college you're interested in, or even a professional who has followed a similar path.

Be careful when choosing a mentor: The fact that someone has been successful in their own journey doesn't mean they are the right person to guide you. Instead of looking for someone who only wants to teach you how to follow in their footsteps, find someone who will help you make your own.

You have the option of taking the Preliminary SAT/National Merit Scholarship Qualifying Test (PSAT/NMSQT). Still, if you take it in 10th grade, you'll have to retake it as a junior to qualify for the National Merit Scholarship Program if you will have a standard 4-year high school career. So you may want to go for the PSAT 10, which will be highly similar. However, if you will be graduating early to enroll in college, you'll want to take the test sophomore year because the award will be offered at the end of your junior year as you finish school. Jump to the eleventh-grade section for more info on this exam or chapter 2 for other testing information.

You're likely still finding what drives you at this point, and there's still plenty of time to experiment. By the time you have a fully-formed transcript, both you and college admissions officers should be able to see what subjects you prioritized. This may be your signature as you enter your next academic chapter, but colleges don't necessarily prefer students who know what they want before even moving into their dorm room. So many people don't find their passion until college or even after.

Now is a great time to start getting in the habit of monitoring your time. Organizers are great tools for that; you can list your daily and weekly activities, see how your days are broken down, and figure out how much time you'll need to plan to devote to specific activities and responsibilities, including work and study. Depending on how full your days become, scheduling your leisure time could also be beneficial. For some students, formally setting aside time to relax or have fun serves as a reminder that these things are necessary and also ensures that they're factored in. An organizer serves not only to help you manage your time but also to assist in prioritizing the most critical responsibilities. Keep in mind, when I say 'organizer,' this could mean a physical planner that you write in or could be the calendar on your phone. I've always preferred the written version, but regardless of how you do it, practicing time management is vital to your future success.

If you haven't explored the option of visiting college campuses yet, now would be a good time, as would your junior year. There's a lot you can learn from actually stepping foot on school grounds and interacting with students. From my experience, current students are usually pretty open to sharing their experiences with you if they know you're considering applying. Don't limit your visit to just the campus itself. It's important to explore the surrounding town- markets, cafés, shops, and places students go to have fun. You'll be spending a lot of time on and around whatever campus you choose, so make sure you'll be comfortable in those spaces. Get to know the libraries, classrooms, and accommodations, but also try to get a clear impression of the people that occupy them. Colleges aren't made up only of buildings and teachers; how students behave can tell you a lot about campus life so visiting when classes are in session is a great option if you're able. If you know what your major will be, you can visit your department and likely get any questions answered from the faculty, students, or your guide.

Most colleges offer a guide to show you around, but there's also value in exploring the place on your own or with a companion. Try eating at their cafeteria, walking around campus, or talking to random students who might give you advice based on their experiences.

Eleventh Grade

If you're starting here, skim the 9th and 10th-grade sections. You have the needed tools to stand out on your application, so it's time to zone in. Focus your energies on becoming the best student you can be. Hopefully, you've chosen your extracurriculars and have been putting some effort into those as well. If not, don't go crazy but definitely choose something to get involved in. Reference the Extracurriculars section for more tips. As mentioned in the Tenth Grade section, visit as many campuses as possible. Maybe you've already narrowed down your college list, but if not, these visits can often help you make those final cuts.

Standing out doesn't mean being a genius and scoring perfectly on every test. It has more to do with showing that you put forth your best efforts and are always willing to learn, not only in the classroom. You may want to start exploring AP courses if you haven't already and if you've done well in honors courses. Reference chapter 2 for information about AP exams. It would also be an excellent time to begin researching financial aid and the differences between scholarships, grants, loans, etc. Also, jump to chapter 3 to read about making your college list and narrowing it down.

Whether you have figured out what you want to do or are still experimenting with different possibilities, you need to start sending inquiries to various colleges, especially if you're aiming for a scholarship. To qualify for a National Merit Scholarship Program, you must take the PSAT/NMSQT in the fall of 11th grade. Other standardized tests, such as the SAT and ACT, can be taken during spring.

If your school offers a Preliminary SAT/National Merit Scholarship Qualifying Test (PSAT/NMSQT), make good use of it. This qualifies students for the National Merit Scholarship Program. Even if your school doesn't offer this test, you can contact your counselor to discuss the possibility of implementing it, or they can tell you where you can take it. The content and skill level required are the same as the PSAT 10, which can be taken in the spring of your sophomore year. Jump to chapter 2 for more testing information.

Twelfth Grade

If you're starting here, skim the 9th through 11th-grade sections. Things are winding up and down at the same time, and you'll need to find a balance. Use your organizer and prioritize tasks. You still need to focus on your studies, don't let your grades slip. As early as possible, schedule any tests you want to improve your scores on or that you haven't taken but need to, reference chapter 2. But also keep in mind that if you're taking AP courses, you'll need to allow yourself time to prep for those exams as well. Whether you dread it or not, the time has come to submit your applications. Take a deep breath, finalize your college list, and submit those applications. (Chapter 3).

Treat your body as your ally. Seriously, it's amazing what a decent diet can do for your efficiency. Of course, this also goes without saying, but... skip the alcohol, smoking, and any kind of drugs. In addition to the effects that could have on your body and mind, you also want to avoid having to explain your arrest record to potential college matches.

Don't underestimate the importance of your free time. It's easy to get overwhelmed by studies, work, college seeking, and extracurricular activities. It can have a severe impact on your mind and even your body. So whenever you're just hanging out, try to live in the moment and not think of anything else. You are only human after all.

Getting Support

You are not alone in this. Accept the support and encouragement of the people around you, whether that's your family, friends, teachers, counselors, or anyone you know you can rely on. Getting advice from a friend or relative who went to the same college you're applying to- or a similar one- can give you a much better understanding of the school than reading brochures.

When the time comes for you to make campus visits, it's nice to have a friend or relative by your side. Get to know the campus together, observe the students, and openly discuss your thoughts.

2

The Myth of the Bad Test Taker

There's no definitive way to measure intelligence, but colleges need a standardized way to evaluate students and level the playing field in a sense. While more and more schools no longer require test scores, you shouldn't limit your college list to only these schools. At least for the time being, I highly recommend still taking the SAT or ACT, maybe twice to improve your scores. While the ACT and SAT are the most popular of these exams, others such as the recent CLT and TOEFL serve international students. Scoring well gives you a leg up at getting into the university of your choice and can qualify you for a merit-based scholarship. Admissions officers have hundreds to thousands of applications to go through, and you need to grab their attention. Good test scores can help that.

The idea that while gifted, some students are just never going to test well is a persistent myth in the academic world. Unfortunately, this myth has led many students to think that they don't have what it takes to get into college, though they would be great students if they could pass the barrier of standardized testing.

There are several types of tests you should consider. Some of them are well known, while others are more niche and don't apply to every case. Here are some highlights:

Advanced Placement (AP) Test

You can take AP courses as early as 9th grade, but this isn't recommended. It's likely best to start in 10th grade, maybe with a history course, and then dive in a little more in your junior and senior year if you feel comfortable. There are currently 38 courses in the program which are audited by the College Board and need to follow certain curriculum specificities. The ones which are approved get the right to use the AP designation. Colleges and universities may offer placement to students who excel at the final AP examination.

AP classes give students a taste of how college classes work. Even students who don't excel at their AP exams improve their chances of getting accepted in their application. Another advantage of taking an AP course is to earn college credit, which can help later on if you want to skip introductory classes, change majors, transfer to another college, or get a second degree.

Different high schools will offer various AP programs. It's crucial that you get to know which are offered in your school and talk to people who took them to see which options better fulfill your needs. AP programs cover many areas of knowledge, and you have to choose the ones that relate to your future career.

SAT

The SAT is offered seven times per year on Saturdays and takes three hours with a few short breaks. You'll need to create a College Board account in order to register. The registration fee is currently $55. Your total score will range between 400 to 1,600. The first section includes a reading test and another portion for writing and language. After that, the math portion is divided into sections where you can use a calculator and another without it.

The test mixes in some science-themed questions, but there isn't a formal science section.

The English and language section is multiple choice, with 44 questions completed within 35 minutes. Then, you'll have 65 minutes to complete the 52-question, multiple-choice reading section focusing on the author's tone. The exam topics may include current events, history, literature, and science.

The essay section has become optional and only available if your school offers it; few students still take it. If you do, you'll have 50 minutes to do so. You'll start by reading a passage between 650 and 750 words. Then you'll be asked to write an essay analyzing the author's argument. You're critiquing the author's writing without inserting your own opinions.

The fact that you're allowed to use a calculator on the first part of your math test doesn't mean you don't need to sharpen your analytical mind. With only 25 minutes to answer 20 questions, you need to think fast and be skillful with the calculator. After that, you have 55 minutes to finish 38 more questions without the help of your little friend.

The questions will cover algebra, geometry, trigonometry, problem-solving, and data analysis. Fourteen total questions within the math section are called the 'Passport to Advanced Math topics and are intended to prepare you to deal with advanced statistics and calculus. You'll sometimes get a fully formed equation and must work backward to find the question that leads to it.

ACT

The ACT is also offered seven times a year on a Saturday by a nonprofit organization of the same name. It has four sections divided into math, English, science, and reading, with the option for a 40-minute writing test. Each subject is scored separately, and the final result is a composition of all of them. The writing section has no impact on that score.

The math section is comprised of 60 multiple-choice questions to be answered in 60 minutes, some of which use a calculator. Topics may include algebra I, algebra II, geometry, and trigonometry.

The English section will have 75 multiple-choice questions with 45 minutes to complete. Highlights include grammar, punctuation, sentence structure, and rhetorical skills.

Unlike the SAT, the ACT does have a fully-formed science section. However, it doesn't necessarily require much scientific knowledge. Instead, it really focuses on how you interpret information and highlights your problem-solving and analysis skills. These 40 multiple-choice questions have to be answered in 35 minutes.

The reading portion of the exam consists of 40 multiple-choice questions with a 35-minute time limit and focuses more on the content of the passages than the reading section of the SAT does.

The writing section asks you to read a passage about a current event and analyze it according to a specific point of view. The goal isn't for you to be a specialist on the discussed subject but to verify your ability to reinterpret the written passage.

Your scores will probably improve if you take the SAT, ACT, or both at least twice. This will help you learn what type of questions/sections you'll need to work on improving. The SAT and ACT are very similar, and you can take practice tests that are free to download from www.act.org and www.collegeboard.org. Taking the PSAT or PreACT is also a fantastic option.

Classic Learning Test (CLT)

While still a novelty, the CLT offers the advantage of taking the test online, with scores divulged on the same day as the exam. The primary issue with the CLT is that it's not recognized by most colleges, finding a home mostly in Christian schools and colleges, including Catholic and Protestant schools as well as some liberal art schools.

CLTs are an excellent option for young people with an unorthodox educational background, such as homeschooling. The test dates are also more flexible, with several monthly exams. The cost to enroll is $54. There are 3 sections: Verbal Reasoning, Grammar/Writing, and Quantitative Reasoning- all scored out of 40.

Test of English as a Foreign Language (TOEFL)

The TOEFL is a standardized test that verifies if a non-native English speaker has enough knowledge of the language to be able to attend and perform well at an English-based college. The test is usually administered in a school building, but that has been changing since the COVID-19 pandemic, and most people prefer to take the test online.

During the three-hour exam, the goal is to determine if the student can perform well in speaking, reading, listening, and writing in English. You will listen to English audio and answer multiple choice questions. There are reading and speaking portions; you may have a conversation with the proctor, or your verbal responses may be recorded.

General Educational Development (GED)

Students who didn't traditionally complete high school can always get their GED. The test covers four subjects (science, social studies, mathematical reasoning, and Reasoning Through Language Arts). Not only does this test offer high school diploma equivalency, but it also grants the student the opportunity to apply for college.

You can register online, but be aware the fee varies between about $80 and $144 depending on the state. To pass, you need a score of 145. But a score of 165 is needed to indicate that you are college ready. If you score 175 or higher, you could potentially earn college credit.

Exam Preparation

FYI, this will mainly be focused on the ACT and SAT exams.

Your performance will depend on several factors, but it helps a lot to know how the exams work. It's important that you take the preliminary versions, if possible, before deciding which one better fits your needs. Usually, when someone takes both preliminary exams to compare, it becomes apparent which one is best for them.

It would be best if you didn't approach these exams quite the same way you would a regular high school test. Instead, you'll perform best with special preparation. Think of it like driving a car for the first time on the day of your driver's license exam. You could pass, but you'll feel more relaxed and execute better if you've practiced. It takes more than knowing the material to excel at a standardized test: You need to familiarize yourself with how it works.

You can buy prep books with exercises from previous versions of the exam or download such versions on the ACT and College Board websites. If you're taking them at home, you should attempt to simulate the same conditions you'll have on the day of the actual test. For example, have a desk in a quiet place with your phone off. Take the tests during the same window of time you'll have on the big day, only using the calculator when permitted and minimizing bathroom breaks.

Ideally, you'll do this ritual every one to two weeks in the three months that lead to the test. This will get you used to the structure and condition your mind to give the best performance under these conditions.

After taking the test, check your answers and grade yourself. You'll soon be able to see what areas you may need to put some study time into. The goal is progress, not perfection. There will always be something you can improve on. Take as many practice exams as you can.

Each person works in their own rhythm, but once you have decided on a plan, a period of 3–4 months should be enough to prepare for the exam. Be careful not to overdo it; always reserve time for leisure, exercise, and other work.

When applying for the SAT or ACT, you're offered the opportunity to send your scores to a few colleges for free. Or, if you'd like to wait and see your scores first, you can send them after you've tested, but for a fee.

Many colleges don't even use the system of test scores anymore. They believe that test performance doesn't represent the overall merit of the student. For many reasons, a strong student might not perform well on a specific test. However, unless you are 100% certain that you will only be applying to schools that do not require test scores (which I don't recommend), you should plan to take the SAT or ACT.

SAT and ACT exams are not just a regurgitation of the content that you've learned in school. Questions can be tricky, designed to show whether you can take everything you've learned in class to the next level. The goal isn't to verify if you remember what was taught in class but if you can employ it in different situations.

They will test the sharpness of your reading speed and ability to interpret the text. Can you understand what the question is asking, with all its nuances? Do you know the subject well enough to make your own conclusions and develop the proper solution? And are you able to handle the pressure of answering all of those questions in a short period? These are the real questions you're being asked.

The Day of the Exam

Since the exam is taken at a specific time and date and in a particular place, many variables can influence your performance. For example, if you get caught in traffic and only arrive at the last minute before doors are closed, your stress level will be much higher than a student who was there on time. Or maybe something in your personal life is distracting you from giving your best. Of course, there's no way of predicting this kind of thing, but it's possible to minimize the chances of them happening with the proper preparation.

Have everything prepared for the day of the exam. This starts with visiting the exam site prior to the day of, if possible. If not, arrive early to allow extra time in case of wrong turns. Be sure you have reliable transportation. Dress in light layers that can adapt to varying weather and thermostat settings. Have your photo ID, no. 2 pencils with fresh erasers, your admission ticket, and an acceptable calculator- you can check collegboard.com to make sure yours is okay. Pens are not allowed on the SAT and ACT exams. You may also want to bring a water bottle and snacks, but you'll only be allowed to consume them during breaks. Remember that you won't be allowed to have your phone, tablet, or any type of camera.

Be in bed on time or even early the night before, and set your alarm with enough time to wake up normally and not feel rushed. We're all guilty of skipping breakfast, but PLEASE eat the morning of the exam. You don't want distracting hunger pangs in the middle of the test, but you don't want to feel heavy either.

The first part of the test you'll encounter is the test instructions. Read them twice; the last thing you want is to make a mistake because of a technicality. So read each question quickly but thoroughly before approaching the answer.

Don't worry about other students moving faster or slower than you. Forget about them and push aside any concerns you may have outside of the exam. Later will handle itself. If you feel too much weight on your shoulders, close your eyes and count to 10, breathing slowly. Then, go back to the test—one question at a time, one section at a time, and so on.

Between the reading and writing sections, you'll get a 10-minute break. Then you'll have another five minutes between the math no-calculator and calculator sections. Use that time wisely-rehydrate, snack, take a bathroom break, and breathe deeply. Push out any lingering thoughts of the previous section of the test before moving on to the next. Once you've completed a section, there's no reason to deplete any brain power continuing to think about it.

Don't despair if some of the questions seem too difficult. Sometimes, the answer is hidden in a minor detail. Move at a good pace by answering the questions you find to be easiest first, then work your way into the more challenging until you have replied to them all. This is not a race against anyone around you; you only need to finish within the allotted timeframe. It's important to answer every question, even if you are unsure. Guessing at an answer is better than leaving it blank. A guess could be correct; a blank will always be wrong.

If there is time after you've finished, reread the whole section, answer by answer, not questioning yourself but just double checking. You may make changes; you may not. That's one of the reasons why these tests are always taken in pencil, not ink. And since you're there, ensure each answer is marked correctly according to the instructions.

So what should you do if you haven't finished your test when the proctor declares five minutes remain? This shouldn't be a cause for despair, but you must be strategic. Once again, it's better to go through the more straightforward remaining questions, the ones you will most likely finish before those five minutes are over. But if you still have quite a few blanks, take some really quick guesses or just mark 'C.' Don't leave blanks.

SAT and ACT exams take around three hours, plus intervals. When the proctor indicates it's time to put pencils down, do it. It might seem to you that with another 15 seconds, you could finish that last question, but you don't have 15 seconds. If you don't stop at the designated time, that could be grounds for dismissal.

3

On Your Mark, Get Set...

When preparing your college application, many things can go right or wrong. In this chapter, I'd like to talk about choosing where to apply, including how to select your top choices and backup options. Take advantage of all the resources at your disposal, including college counselors, teachers, and advisers who can provide you with advice and letters of recommendation.

While there may not be only one right decision here, your college choice is important. Not only will you spend your next few years in this school, but its name and reputation could follow you afterward. So don't settle for the easiest one to get into, but don't underestimate less demanding colleges either, including community colleges. It's not always easy to find the place you fit into, but let's do our best.

Selecting the Right College

You might be too young to remember a time when the internet wasn’t intertwined with our entire lives, but that was true once. Nowadays, you have this fantastic tool at your disposal. So sit down and spend some time building a list of universities that offer what you're looking for. There are thousands to choose from across the United States, but you'll aim to build a list of about twenty to twenty-five and narrow it down from there.

Every school has a website that allows you to compare them according to their location, courses, and whatever else matters to you as a potential student. In addition, it can clue you in on what schools value in a student so that you know what aspects of your schooling and personal life you may want to focus on or so that you can go ahead and cross them off your list.

Organize your list of potential colleges in order of preference. You should have some amount of attraction to the ones at the bottom, and your dream school will be at the top. Classify your list according to factors such as location, your desired major, extracurriculars you’re interested in, class sizes, and anything else that matters to you. Decide the importance of these factors as you see them personally. It may even be helpful to have multiple lists with your college choices organized by each category.

Just because you've never heard of a school doesn't mean it couldn't be right for you. You may flourish the most at a little known university. Research beyond the ones highlighted in the media, and you'll get to know great new places that might have exactly what you're looking for. You may find a school that flows beautifully with your fiercely unique self, but you didn't even know it existed. You are in the driver's seat, completely in charge of carving your life path and deciding where you want to do it. Don't stop looking after you've checked ten or even fifty schools. It's worth spending significant time on this.

Of course, each college's webpage will only highlight the positives. Still, you can find plenty of helpful information: weather conditions, class size, location/distance from your home, activities (sports, theater, social issues), and cost. That information will allow you to eliminate a good chunk of colleges from your list immediately or pop them up near the top of your list.

Corsava.com is a good resource to help you find the right college. They offer the Corsava Card Sort, a tool that matches you with the right school according to how you rank certain characteristics. You'll choose one of four options for each factor: Must Have, Would Be Nice, Do Not Care, and No Way. You respond to each factor according to your needs and expectations, and they will compare it to their database, offering personalized results.

You can also try out collegedata.com, specifically their College Chances section. They'll analyze your grades, test scores, extracurriculars, and other factors to approximate your chances of getting into certain schools.

Around 40% of high schools use Naviance. If yours doesn't, check it out anyway. It's a great resource for helping you through the college application process and may affect where you choose to apply.

You can tell a lot about a college by the way they work through their admission process. If all they require is a transcript and test scores, they want students comfortable with independence and self-advocacy. However, if they also asks for supplemental essays, letters of recommendation, and interviews, you'll need to be prepared for more class participation and relationship development with faculty and staff.

After you've built your list or lists based on how you match with each college according to your preferences, you'll want to find out which of them you can truly afford. Before considering applying, contact each college's financial aid office and ask about their programs. Information about their processes and deadlines will be valuable in case you get accepted. Remember that the average cost of attendance that schools post on their website is meant to be an example of the maximum price you should expect to pay. If you can be more frugal than average when it comes to your social life and transportation costs (not to mention any scholarships), you won't be paying a bill that high. Also be aware that some states have agreements with the states surrounding them, allowing students to pay in-state tuition without being a state resident. While thinking about this, keep in mind that some scholarship deadlines will come before you even know which schools you've been accepted to. Point being, don't put off scholarship research and application- the summer before your senior year even.

Once you have your list ready—or even half ready—it's time to schedule a one-on-one meeting with your school counselor to discuss possibilities. They'll be able to provide more insight as this won't be their first rodeo. They may even have some suggestions of schools you left off your list. Use all your resources to thoughtfully narrow down your list to the top eight or so. Again, number one would be your dream school, and near the bottom would be a few schools that are basically sure things but that you'd also enjoy attending. Include choices on your list that are difficult to get into, but be sure that your list also includes schools with a sixty percent or so acceptance rate or better. You don't want to bet your future on the chance of getting into a school that admits less than ten percent of applicants with no Plan B or C. This could lead to a lot of unnecessary stress or could even delay beginning your college experience altogether.

Regular and Rolling Admissions vs. Early Decision (ED) and Early Action (EA)

You may choose to apply to college via regular decision or rolling admissions. If you want to have your application reviewed in a specific time frame, you need to apply for regular decision. At the same time, rolling admissions are judged on a rolling basis, in the order that each candidate's application was received. You might also choose to join a pool of students who get their applications in early.

With ED, you can only apply this way to one college, and in case you are selected, you'll need to withdraw all applications you made to other schools. They're usually due in November, even though some colleges have earlier deadlines or may offer additional rounds in fall and winter.

With EA, you can apply to several colleges, and you are not bound to study at the one that accepts you. This is different from Restrictive Early Action (REA), which is also nonbinding but doesn't allow you to apply to any binding programs simultaneously. Both EA and REA are also due in November.

Before applying for ED, ask yourself if that college is and should be at the top of your list. If accepted, would you go without hesitation? Be sure you've researched that school thoroughly, leaving no room for doubt. That means not only checking out their website but also visiting the campus and testing out the accommodations. Talk to current and former students online or in person. You need to be sure you know what life will be like on that campus. Also, check that you can afford the tuition and familiarize yourself with their financial aid program to avoid getting caught by surprise.

Demonstrated Interest

Demonstrated interest goes beyond stating that you want to study at a specific school. You have to say it through action as well. This process involves taking direct and efficient measures to show you are prepared and excited to start your academic life there. This process must be done for each school separately, so you should direct your efforts only at your completed college list, the top four or so. You don't want to waste time doing this for dozens of schools. Also, be sure that the ones you choose to put this labor toward actually track DI. That being said, demonstrating interest is absolutely not required. You'll still be considered as an applicant if you do nothing but apply.

That doesn't mean you are crossing the other ones off the list. You're still likely to get accepted into a university in which you haven't demonstrated interest. They'll read your application and base their decision on other factors, such as your grades and test scores. You never know, demonstrating interest may be the tie-breaker if a school needs to make a final decision between you and another student.

A student that demonstrates interest will make the life of the admissions officer easier, at least for the schools that track DI. When selecting future students, admissions officers want to ensure they are offering spots to people who are interested in accepting rather than wasting their time and effort with those who aren't serious.

The most direct and effective way of demonstrating interest is to call the admissions representative and introduce yourself and asking specific question about a program or something similar that can't easily be found online. You can schedule a virtual meeting to talk about your prospects and aspirations. Writing a polite and eloquent email can work just as well, just make sure you send it to the right person. It's sometimes as simple as googling '*insert college here* region rep.' In either case, try not to overdo it: If you send them a message daily or even weekly, it becomes annoying.

Another direct way of showing interest in a college is by visiting and getting to know people who study and work there. The admissions officers will take note of your activity, whether you attended or canceled a scheduled visit. If you cannot show up on the scheduled date, make sure you cancel it with a couple of days' notice, optimally rescheduling for another time.

There are other more subtle ways of demonstrating interest. For example, when you take the time to read the emails sent from the school, you show that you care about the content. Colleges may be notified when you open an email or especially when you click on a link; that data will show that you are serious in your pursuit of acceptance to that school. On the subject of technology, follow the school's social media pages, like the Instagram posts, react to the Facebook posts, retweet to your heart's content.

Admissions officers often travel to attend high school fairs where they talk to students about their prospects. If you have the chance to participate in one of these events, ask them for an inquiry card so that you can provide your information and express your interest in their school. It might seem like a small gesture, but college admissions officers hold on to these cards to keep track of potential students.

Letters of Recommendation

Admissions officers appreciate letters of recommendation from teachers and other professionals. They tell the part of the story that the transcript doesn't. That could mean how much the student participates in class, their relationship with their peers, and leadership qualities, among other things.

Admission letters are most effective when they come from someone you've formed a good relationship with-teachers, peers, mentors. This can also be helpful if you have a disciplinary violation on your record and want an opportunity to share the details and how you dealt with it. A well-spoken teacher, counselor, coach, boss, etc., may be able to intercede in your favor. Even a religious leader or volunteer coordinator can write the letter.

A teacher's only compensation for writing a recommendation letter is to help students fulfill their potential. Their schedule is likely already busy, so be respectful of that; Be prepared and grateful if they are willing to take the time to write it for you. Request the letter within a reasonable time frame so they can write it without pressure. The sooner, the better, seriously. Three weeks before the application deadline should be the absolute latest. Even the beginning of the school year is not too soon.

It can be tricky to pick the right person to request a letter from. Teachers are a great choice, not only because of their area of expertise but because they are in close contact with you during the school year. They'll often know you personally and may even teach a subject you excel at, or that is related to your major. But don't rule out teachers from classes you didn't do your best in. Did you push yourself to get that B? Your teacher likely saw that effort and can speak to it.

During your junior year, start thinking about who you'd like to ask for a letter of recommendation, narrowing your list to the two to three people you think will be the best fit. You can request that letter in many ways, but face-to-face is always the best option. If that's not possible, you can write them a polite email, citing your reasons for picking them and your plans for the future. Don't be too formal, but be respectful, and end with a 'thank you.'

Recommendation letters can vary in tone and quality. The best ones will praise you while still being realistic about your accomplishments. A letter that paints you as a perfect genius can be as harmful as one that details all your flaws.

High school teachers and counselors have hundreds of students, so they can't be expected to remember everything about you. When requesting the letter, try to refresh their memory about your accomplishments, citing specific incidents that illustrate your qualities. Also, any test scores or transcripts your chosen author may not have access to. You may need to have a few conversations or exchange emails with the letter-writer between your initial request and the letter delivery. Always be polite and friendly without fawning. Keep all emails professional, well-formatted, and free of errors.

After the letter is finished and you've submitted it for consideration, keep the teacher informed of your application steps. You certainly don't have to email them about it every day, but it's nice to let them know if you were successful or not. In either case, thank them for their time and effort, and let them know how much you appreciate all their effort.

Working With Counselors

School counselors are professionals trained to help students go through the application process. In U.S. high schools, advisers are usually overloaded with work, assigned to hundreds of students every year. As a result, some can only meet with their counselors once a year and for a short period. In most cases, counselors spend less time dealing with students' college applications and more on other responsibilities.

One meeting might not be enough, but you have to make the best of it if that's all you can schedule. When you talk to your counselor, be open about your school life, your history, and what you want for your future. This is valuable time spent, and you should be honest, even if you have no idea of how you want to proceed. After you tell them about who you are and what you want to do, you should discuss your options. Don't be afraid to respectfully reject their suggestions if they don't fit your goals. That's part of the process, and this discussion will help you pave the path toward what you want. This session is not a test but a useful tool. You will not get a grade by the end of it, and you will not fail if you don't figure everything out right then and there.

Parents often have a clear idea of what they want for their children, which may or may not be the best thing for them. The school counselor's evaluation may not match the career or college choices your parents envisioned. That's not necessarily bad, even though parents are often displeased with these conclusions. Ultimately you should consider both parties' advice, but the choices are yours. Sometimes a counselor's job is to be the bearer of bad news. If they think that a particular college is not the right fit for you or that attending a university may not be the right choice for you at all, it's their job to tell you. That can sound like an insult, but it isn't. It might be your parents' dream that you become a doctor or an engineer, but if your transcript says you're more talented with history than biology or math, maybe you should consider a different path. This process isn't meant just to help you find the ideal career but also the ideal college to get you there. The system isn't perfect, and there's always the chance the 'best' place for you doesn't fit your budget.

You and your family are free to disagree and veer in a different direction. Just keep in mind that the counselor's recommendation isn't a mere guess. They are educated professionals with a deeper knowledge of the field, and you should consider what they say, even if you don't ultimately follow their advice.

The school counselor's job is to guide you, but you'll still have to do much of the work yourself. That means researching courses, campus visits if possible, demonstrating interest, making travel arrangements, and getting all the needed documentation and transcripts ready by the required deadlines. If you have enough resources, you do have the option of hiring an independent college adviser. This professional will walk you through the many steps of college admission. Unlike your school's counselor, who deals with an entire student population, the independent adviser will offer individualized assistance according to your needs. Apart from picking the right college, the independent adviser will also guide you through the process of planning your school life, including organizing your extracurricular activities. They'll also help you to prepare for interviews, apply for financial aid, and improve your demonstrated interest efforts.

There are many independent college advisers out there, and choosing one can be tricky. It's okay to ask for advice from a friend or relative with personal experience; just be aware that's not the same as hiring a professional. When hiring an adviser, I'd recommend choosing someone with at least three years of experience working with high school students. Check to see if they're members of the National Association for College Admission Counseling (NACAC) or Independent Educational Consultants Association (IECA). Members of these organizations have proven professional experience, guaranteeing they have worked with students in the past. Your private adviser should be proactive, keeping up to date with academic life. If they are unable to answer some of your questions, they should be able to tell you who can.

Now keep in mind that the private adviser is only as good as their client: You'll have to combine forces to reach your desired outcome. Beware of those who promise 100% certainty that you will get into your dream school. You don't want to work with someone who is just going to tell you what you want to hear. If you suspect your adviser is not being honest with you or that they are doing something unethical, you should look elsewhere before they damage your prospects. You likely won't interact with someone who blatantly offers to write an essay for you or suggests bribing an admissions officer, but some shady goings-on can be packaged in a much less obvious way. Remember that participating in such things could damage everything you've fought so hard for.

4

Go!

In this chapter, we'll go through the process of completing your application, apart from essay writing. For essay info, jump to Chapter 5. Here we're going to discuss how to prepare for and perform in an interview, what admissions officers look for in a candidate, and how to create an appealing list of activities.

Admissions officers (AOs) go through thousands of applications over a few months, so it's best to stand out from the beginning. Believe it or not, AOs will generally only spend a few minutes on each application due to the enormous amount they have to get through. There's no magic formula, but there are guidelines that will help you figure out what to do and—just as important—what not to do.

The Interview

Not every college offers interviews for prospective students. If you get the chance to give an interview, it will be either informational or evaluative. Informational interviews serve as a 'get-to-know-you.' They may not impact the admission decision, unlike evaluative interviews. These interviews are opportunities for admissions officers to get a better feel for who you are and help them to decide whether their university is a good match for you. I think I should also mention, do not bring your parents.

The admissions officer often conducts evaluative interviews. This won't be the deciding factor in their decision, but it will certainly matter. If you are offered the chance to do an interview, make the best of the opportunity- it's a good way to demonstrate interest.

Interviews are about the human factor of a prospective student. The admissions officer already has your grades, test scores, and transcripts. Now, they want to know the person behind that data. You'll talk about your interests, hopes, and ambitions and decide together if that college is right for you. They may want to know about the books you like to read, what movies you watch, what you consider your most significant accomplishment, the people you admire the most, how you expect to evolve during your academic life, etc. Feel free to elaborate. AOs aren't looking for just the title of the book or a person's name. The questions are meant to help them discover something about you, how you think- your passions.

Schedule your interview as far in advance as you feel comfortable. This will allow you time to develop and rehearse a few responses to the most common questions and also to research the school.

Bring your resume to the interview- include skills, accomplishments, work history, and anything you think may be beneficial to have handy. The process of writing the resume will prepare you for the interview as well.

If possible, visit the place where you'll have the interview beforehand to avoid getting lost on the way there. Being late isn't a good look, so plan to arrive at least 10 minutes before the interview. There's no need to wear a suit, but avoid jeans and T-shirts. Business casual is likely the way to go.

Stay calm. Be prepared to answer questions regarding a poor grade or any disciplinary issues. Be honest, explain yourself, and express what you learned from it.

Vague questions can be the hardest to answer. You may be asked comprehensive questions or prompts such as 'Tell me about yourself." You'll want to have something prepared in order to respond appropriately. Don't feel intimidated by this and try to avoid clichés and over-simplified answers, such as "I try to be a good person." Instead, focus on your accomplishments and the things you're most proud of. Be honest about your strengths and weaknesses. This isn't just about what subjects you're best at but also about how you've learned to overcome challenges.

AOs may also ask why you want to pursue the particular major you've chosen. Again, the time you've spent researching the school will pay off. One main factor in accepting a new student is determining how they will contribute to academic and student life. Not only are they looking for someone who will be a good student, but also someone who will have a positive impact socially.

One rather tricky question might come is some variation of "where do you see yourself in ten years?" They are not asking you to predict the entire course of your career but instead want to see if you are able to think ahead in the long term- if you have any sort of game plan or goals. Don't limit your answer to your professional life; describe where you think you'll be regarding relationships and commitment to your interests.

Colleges are not looking for students with a perfect history; that would actually be suspicious. Each student has to be able to stand out for their own reasons. This also works the other way around. One great college isn't going to be the right place for every student. The whole point of the admission process is to determine if each is a good fit for the other.

You'll want to avoid asking obvious questions about the college, such as ones whose answers can easily be found on their website. But don't be afraid to ask tough questions. Matters such as student loans, alumni employability, and campus security can't be overlooked. You're allowed to ask for official data. By doing this, you may even show that you're serious about the school and display your attention to detail.

At the end of the interview, ask if they have a business card so you can keep in touch. Then, send a follow-up thanking them for the opportunity, and let them know you're available to answer any further questions.

Informational interviews also allow you to get to know more about the school. Interviewers—usually alumni or current college students—are open to questions and will help ease any of your concerns. They've likely gone through the same process, so you can expect them to be friendly and well-intentioned. This interview will serve as a communication channel between the college and you. Informational interviews present their own challenges. These alumni are prepared to provide you with positive insight into academic life.

Alumni interviews are valuable for anyone applying to Ivy League colleges. Other universities may consider them an important factor in accepting new students or a mere formality. Either way, you want to give a good impression, so follow the same guidelines as the evaluative interview: Don't be late, dress neatly, stay calm, be polite, and ask for a business card at the end.

Remember that you are not the only one who needs to make a good impression. The alumni interview is your chance to find out if this college is really suited for you. Be prepared to ask the tough questions; if the answers aren't satisfactory, you might have to reconsider your application to that university.

The person interviewing you has seen all sides of the school during their student years. The school has selected them as a representative, and you can expect them to praise all of its qualities. But they should also be honest about their time there and are expected to be truthful. This will be a casual conversation, but there's still a degree of formality. The alumnus is volunteering for the job and wants to find new people who can add value to their beloved alma mater.

The interviewer will already be familiar with you in the way an AO would. They might ask questions about your high school years, goals, and social life or extracurricular activities, but they will also be interested in your interpersonal skills.

Take the opportunity to ask the interviewer about their life on campus, including significant or interesting events, accommodations, transportation, and facilities. You can also ask about their favorite professors and the majors you're interested in. You might find out that you and your interviewer have a lot in common. Some students keep in touch with these alumni and find that they're great mentors moving forward.

Still, be careful not to get too friendly and reveal personal details that could make a bad impression. The goal here is still to find out if you will be a valuable asset to the school and if it can fulfill your academic needs in return, so I'd hesitate to ask about frat parties and related things. After the interview, the alumnus may or may not prepare a report detailing their impressions and conclusions for the admissions officer. This will vary by school.

The Common App and Short Answers

Give the Common Application a shot. It's an online system through which you can simultaneously apply to over 900 colleges and universities. This way, you'll only have to enter your general information once. It even allows you to apply to colleges in Canada, China, Japan, and many European countries.

Some universities will require short answer questions. You may have space for three, fifteen, or fifty words. Whatever room you're given, use what's available to elaborate on your answers; responses should not be one or two words. Keep them confined to the specified word count while also showing your personality; these questions are still meant as an opportunity to allow the reader a peek into your head, heart, and soul. Show your wit and intelligence, and use the limited word count to your advantage. Try not to choose the obvious responses. Be specific and present new information when you can; don't simply regurgitate what's already elsewhere on your application or resume. And just like your essays, try to sound natural, like you're sitting in a coffee shop making a new friend. Do not be afraid to go with the humorous response.

If an acquaintance asks "What's your favorite food?" would you only say "lasagna."? I doubt it. You'd likely expand on that. Is it specifically your grandmother's lasagna? Did you grow up eating it? Did she teach you how to make the noodles by hand? Have you built an emotional connection to the smell of the tomato sauce simmering? Now you've allowed a glimpse into your family life, your psyche even. It's personal; there's more meaning behind it.

Eleven Mistakes to Avoid on Your Application

Knowing what to do to get into college is just as important as knowing what to avoid. Each case has its own nuances, but I've developed a list of 11 mistakes that I believe are some of the most common errors people make while preparing that application. So here's a list of the *Do-Nots* that could make or break your chance of acceptance:

1.**Don't ignore directions**

I had a math teacher in middle school that would frequently include instructions on quizzes and tests that made no sense: 5 extra credit points for writing your favorite color at the top of the quiz, sign your name across the left margin of this page. I remember one particular exam vividly. The directions at the top of the first page instructed us to skip the entire second page of questions. I glanced at the second page just out of curiosity and realized the difficulty of the problems was more advanced than what I and my fellow classmates were prepared to answer. It was pretty easy to look around and determine which students had not read the directions based on the confused looks on their faces. My teacher wanted to be sure we always took the time to read instructions, long, short, silly, or rationale.

Each school you apply to will have directions on how to proceed with your application. Reading those instructions only takes a few minutes and could make a world of difference down the line. It's the simple things that make a difference sometimes.

The application process varies from school to school, and change can happen in a short period of time. Therefore, it's important to pay attention to the directions and ensure you have the most recent updates. Don't assume that the rules from one school apply to all of them, or you'll waste time submitting an improper application.

2.**Don't let parents do everything; you take the lead.**

Some parents participate more than others in their children's college applications and in their academic life in general. Most help is valuable, but this process concerns you and your future. Would you take either of your parents with you to a job interview? In case it isn't obvious, the answer is a resounding no. If you sit back and let them do all the research and work for your applications, you'll regret it. Some students let their parents take the lead because they're afraid, feel they don't have a choice, or haven't independently approached something as challenging before. If you're unaccustomed to relying on your own abilities, view this process as a rite of passage, learning to advocate for yourself.

3.**Don't turn in an extensive resume**.

At this point in your life, your resume might look a bit slim. If you are still in high school, your work history is probably not too impressive compared to adults. As a result, you may feel that you need to add unnecessary details to bulk it up. Resist that temptation, especially if it makes your resume over one page. Resumes are meant to be concise and easy to read, and it's easier to achieve these things if you keep it short and focus on relevant experiences.

4.**Don't forget to proofread**

The content of your application is most important, but formatting errors will also make an impact on the admissions officer who reviews it. You want to pull them into your story, catch their interest, and make them feel what you feel. Typos, misspelled words, and grammatical errors will take away from your narrative. It will also give the impression that you're sloppy and don't pay attention to detail.

Before submitting any material, you should have it proofread. It's helpful to show it to someone you know and whose opinions you trust so they can pinpoint any mistakes or suggest changes. You don't necessarily have to hire a professional, but getting a second or even third set of eyes on your writing is helpful when trying to polish your work.

5.**Don't wait until the last minute to apply**.

Preparing a college application takes a lot of effort, and you need to make the best of your time. It could take months, even years, to build the foundations for a good application. You have to gather your materials, exchange messages, plan trips, take tests, and organize your finances, to only name a few. Each of these has its own deadlines; the only way to ensure you are doing them right is by taking the time to complete them correctly. This should go without saying: Do not miss deadlines, not even by a matter of minutes.

If you wait until the last minute to get started, you'll realize you've already missed deadlines you didn't even know existed. For instance, lots of scholarships have an application deadline in November, October, even September. Interested applicants will need to get started in the summer before they've even begun their senior year.

6.**Don't repeat yourself**.

Your application should be easy to read. This will help the admissions officers to make their decisions promptly and keep their aggravation to a minimum. Remember, they are reading dozens of applications per day. You might feel the urge to repeat information in order to highlight its significance, especially regarding an accomplishment you're proud of, but that will only make your application monotonous. Plus, you want to fit as much of your life and personality into it as possible.

Think of a newspaper article in which the journalist has to report what they saw in a few words while answering all the questions that the reader might have about that incident. There's no point in saying things more than once; doing so may weaken the text rather than strengthen it.

7.**Don't give colleges unoriginal applications.**

Cookie-cutter applications are not fun to read. They're boring and most definitely don't stand out. They will often come from students who aren't super interested in that particular college, haven't been provided with the appropriate coaching, or haven't been taught how to show their uniqueness and capabilities. If you're the latter, ask yourself what authentically makes you who you are, and try to reflect that in your application. It's okay to reference your obscure hobby or tv show, make a joke or two, and be a little bit playfully irreverent. If that's all part of who you are, then it's great if it shines through in your application.

8. **Don't go overboard with extracurricular activities.**

Extracurricular activities are a crucial part of your application, but quality matters more than quantity. For example, suppose you are playing a sport or an instrument, studying a language, doing volunteer work, writing a blog, learning to decorate cakes, and reading two books per week, all at the same time. In that case, chances are you're not doing them well or with much pleasure or passion. Rather than trying to do too much, you can give your extracurriculars a boost just by describing them in a stronger way. Did you research something or did you investigate, critique, quantify, or extract it? Maybe you established, coordinated, or restructured rather than lead. A quick Google of 'strong verbs' is all it takes. Put these to good use, but don't cross that line into oddity. You still want to sound natural.

Admissions officers are interested in how you manage your time, but that doesn't mean filling each minute of every day with a plethora of activities. It has more to do with finding the time each day to work on something you want to accomplish or you're passionate about. Knowing how to relax and learning the importance of allowing yourself the time to do nothing are skills worth developing too. This is especially true as you're going through the application process. It's much nicer to come out the other side excited for what's next rather than burnt out and only excited for a nap.

9.**Don't forget to check the curriculum requirements.**

Before applying to a college, you should read their curriculum requirements to determine if it's the place for you. While you'll learn a lot from visits and interviews, you need to review the curriculum requirements in order to understand what kind of class load the college expects from students and whether you're prepared to meet that expectation.

The curricula offer an idea of how to follow your chosen path during your college years and what high school courses you need on your transcript to get into your preferred program. They are updated regularly, so you should always look for the most recent version.

10.**Don't overthink.**

Even with all this information thrown at you and so many steps to prepare for, it's best not to overthink the process. The foundation is built by your actions-test scores, grades, and extracurricular participation, and the content you submit will be a reflection of that. Your letter of recommendation will be based on what you've done and what you're capable of doing. Don't lose sleep over your application, your essays, or your interview. You'll perform better if your stress levels are low and if you have a school on two on your list that you have very good chances of acceptance to.

11.**Don't rely entirely on the advice of those who haven't recently been through what you're going through.**

You can learn from the experiences of others, but this journey is uniquely your own. Maybe you know someone who has graduated from your dream college and who's willing to give you advice. Even though their experience is valuable, they can only tell you how the admission process functioned for them, with their background and at the time they applied. But the more recently they applied, the fresher the experience will be in their mind, and the more up-to-date their knowledge will be. The admission process in any college is altered over time. While you can still get precious information from people who have gone through it in the distant past, you shouldn't rely too heavily on this advice as the process has undoubtedly changed.

Keeping a Good Profile

People's lives have become more public than ever, and you need to be aware of the impression you leave during this point in your life, not to mention when you're applying for a job. Admissions officers look for candidates who make a good impression and will only reflect positively on the school if chosen as a student. One of the ways they may verify this is through your presentation, both in person and online.

A good presentation begins with your communication history with the school. If you sent an insulting email at some point, that could influence your chances. You'll be presented with many opportunities to let your personality show, from your interview to how you relate to the college's employees, including secretaries and receptionists.

Schools may look into your social media pages, looking for content that's revealing about your personality. Old offensive tweets and Facebook posts can damage a person's academic or professional life, even if they've evolved and no longer think that way.

You could go back and try eliminating everything embarrassing you've ever posted. The easy alternative is to set your Facebook account on private mode, so only the people in your list of contacts can have access to that material. At times, that may not be enough, and if you are asked to justify what you posted, stay humble and be ready to show them how much you've learned and matured.

Once you're a college student, you are responsible for representing them pretty much wherever you go. Even off campus, you still carry their name. If you get arrested for fighting, using drugs, or driving under the influence, the school's reputation could suffer because of it. They are entitled to disciplinary actions, which could go from a warning to suspension or even expulsion.

This also applies to how you behave on the internet, even once you're accepted. Avoid making rude comments online about the college or its teachers and students, not to mention posting anything racist, sexist, etc. This reflects poorly on you and the university. If you feel a professor isn't fulfilling their duties or you're having issues with another student, reach out to the Office of Student Affairs or your university's equal.

Be careful with the websites you visit while on campus. The computers in the library should be used exclusively for studying and research purposes. You have more freedom when using your laptop in your room, but you shouldn't use the college's internet signal to access anything inappropriate or illegal.

5

Putting the Metaphorical Pen to Paper

In the previous chapter, we went through most of the application process. However, I feel one part deserves its own chapter: essays. This skill of essay writing will prove beneficial not just with your college applications but in the years to come, throughout your academic and professional life. If you opted to take a creative writing course during high school, tune into that knowledge base.

We'll cover the different essay structures and content forms, how to craft and revise the first draft, and the best ways to finish your essay. Like any other part of your application, it needs to grab the AO's attention and display your merits without sounding cocky.

Presenting Yourself

The purpose of the personal essay is to express who you are, what's important to you, and what contribution you could make to the college. Think of it as an interview before the interview. Admissions officers may use it to narrow down the candidates they want to meet in person.

Your essays will be based on prompts. The most common kind of prompt asks why you chose that college among all others. You may also be asked why you're pursuing a specific major or how you relate to the community you came from.

The goal is not to blow smoke up the school's you-know-what. You won't get in just by saying that you want to go there because they are the most incredible college in the world and you've dreamed of attending since you were a baby. That's obviously a very straightforward example, but you get it. Brown-nosing isn't a good look. You also aren't trying to argue that you're a good person or well-liked. You aren't even trying to prove that you're intelligent. Instead, you'll show your merit, personality, and love of the school through your writing and how you express yourself. Are you clever, creative, bold, charming, or careful, planned, organized? You want your writing to reflect your values, your inner thoughts, how you see the world and seemingly ordinary things. Your intellect and likeability will shine through without having to focus too much effort on it.

Remember that while you most definitely want to show the reader who you are, what you value, and where your strengths lie, you want to be sure your writing will still make sense to someone with an average knowledge base of what you're writing about. What I mean is that it's okay to use the jargon associated with your craft in order to show that you know a thing or two about it. Just don't go overboard to the point that it sounds like you're gloating or you isolate the reader. You wouldn't expect someone new to stock trading to follow along and stay engaged in a essay that is chock-full of phrases such as 'volatility', 'liquidity', 'averaging down', or 'public float'.

The essay should be easy to read but also direct and concise. You may choose to craft a long, flourished introduction or get straight to the point, but it's essential to define the main idea of what you're writing one way or another.

When you write an essay about why you chose a particular major, avoid starting with something like, "I've always liked animals, so I think I will be a great veterinarian." This is too simple. If you're basing your essay on this idea, start by brainstorming. While it's vital to showcase some vulnerability, this kind of comment sounds childish and unprofessional.

A good approach is to ask yourself how you plan to contribute in that field. In the veterinarian's case, it could be that you want to work in research or open your own clinic. You can also say that you've been following that market, that its future seems bright, and that you want to be a part of it.

It's possible to write a great essay even if you're unsure of what major you will pursue. Pick one to three that interest you the most and focus your essay on them. Find a correlation between these fields, and use it to your advantage. The process of writing that essay might even help you in your decision afterward.

Some prompts will ask you to write about your relationship with the community. In that case, you should ask yourself what community means to you. It could be where you live and the people who surround you physically, but it could also mean the people you don't have personal contact with but are present in your life by virtual means, such as social networks or causes. You might not know them as individuals but as people who share a belief, such as a religion or a political idea.

Writing About Yourself

You can get into college by writing four to six essays, as long as they're top-notch. For that, you need to pick the appropriate prompts and develop them in the best way possible. Create a spreadsheet with all of your prompts, and brainstorm the ones that you think would be a good fit for your writing style, opinions, and experiences. Of course, you should never lie or distort the truth, but you can make it sound more attractive if you know what you're doing. And storytelling does not necessarily constitute a lie.

Brainstorming prompts is as simple as asking yourself who you are, what you've done, what sets you apart from others, and what is important to you. These fundamental questions can lead to unexpected results. What are you most proud of? What smell do you associate good feelings or memories with? What's something important you've learned that you didn't know only a short time ago? What is your love language and why do you think that is? Write down the answers, and give yourself the freedom to deviate from them, at least at this stage in the process.

These prompts will ask you to write about yourself. Honesty is important, but you should also know what schools expect from prospective students. Ask yourself what your basic characteristics are, which ones you'd like to change, and the things you are proud of. Putting all of that onto paper will make you look at things differently.

Your personality was molded by the events of your life. Decide which ones made the most significant impact on who you are. Then, make a timeline to determine what happened, when, and the consequences. A month is a reasonable amount of time to write your personal statement, which you might say is the most important essay of the bunch.

The first thing you have to do is analyze the prompt you're going to write about. In some cases, you'll have the option to choose among several prompts. This doesn't mean that some are easier than others, and some people actually prefer not being given options. This could stimulate your creativity by forcing you to elaborate on the only option you're given. This will also keep you from deciding to switch prompts in the middle of the writing process, which can be very counterproductive.

After you're given or have decided on your prompt, try starting by underlining its keywords. This will help you to zone in on what you're really writing about and identify what is being asked of you.

Another good exercise to stimulate your creativity is to do some freewriting. Open your computer and start writing about the prompt without overthinking or stopping. Your writing doesn't have to be good at this point, it hardly needs to be on topic. Doing this exercise for half an hour to an hour could awaken ideas you didn't realize were there and give you some jumping-off points to play with. When you come back to read it, make notes and highlight the ideas that deserve to be developed.

You can consider your outline to be the zero draft of your essay. This should roughly specify what each paragraph will look like. Then you can start with draft one.

Writing the first draft can be challenging and demand the most of your creativity. Keep in mind that first drafts are never perfect; they're rarely even good! However, you have to write them to have something to edit later on. Even the world's greatest writers struggle with their first drafts, and you are no exception.

After you finish this draft, go back and be sure that you addressed everything asked of you in the prompt. Don't despair if you find a lot of mistakes or haven't answered all the questions initially. Once you're sure the prompt has been fully responded to, then go through and do your reorganizing, rewriting, deleting, additions, adding more of your personality (or less if really needed), all that jazz. Don't expect your second draft to be the final draft, or even close. There is not necessarily a number of drafts to shoot for, just write and edit until you're happy with the essay.

Now, set it aside for a few days, then come back with fresh eyes. Reading your essay out loud can also give you a new perspective on your work. Finish by checking for spelling, grammar, and formatting errors. You can use spell check, apps like Grammarly, and those around you whose grammatical skills you trust.

The personal essay will reveal a lot about who you are, not just through the story you're telling but also through the quality of your writing. Your language should be simple, direct, and not overly formal or too casual.

Standing Out with your Essay

A person who has the habit of reading will be better equipped to write any kind of text. Fiction authors tend to show the vulnerability of their characters to make the reader feel what these make-believe people are experiencing. That's a quality you also want to convey in your essay. These, together with your core values, will flesh out your personality for the person reading the essay.

An essay should be easy to read and never dull. A great way to start an essay is with an anecdote. Present the story of a moment in your life that relates to the contents of the piece, and begin to develop it from there. You shouldn't aim to just pick any story that will gain sympathy from the admissions officer. Instead, write about something that will demonstrate the qualities they are looking for in a candidate.

Whether you have already decided on a major or not, try to be specific when discussing your college aspirations. Many students make the mistake of trying to sound like jacks-of-all-trades, with so many goals and ambitions that could only be obtained in two lifetimes. Admissions officers may view that more as indecisiveness than passion, or it may just make it seem like you're not being honest.

The end of your essay will give the admissions officer a lasting impression. Simplicity goes a long way. You have written an entire piece about the experiences that molded you into who you are, and it's time to bring it full circle. It's a good idea to convey how much you've grown and how much you hope to keep growing in the future as new challenges and opportunities show up.

Proofreading, Revising, and Editing

Submitting an essay with grammar, punctuation, or formatting mistakes can significantly detract from how powerful your application may be, even with otherwise brilliant content. Of course, writing skills aren't something you acquire in one day, and your chances will be better if you pay attention in English class. But writing a few practice essays and getting input from your peers can help those skills to evolve quickly.

Some quick pointers for revisions and edits:

Walk away- take breaks, especially when you're getting frustrated. You'll be surprised how much easier it may be to get your thoughts in order or find mistakes when you've let that part of your brain rest for a bit.

Read your essay out loud- does it sound natural? If not, it probably needs some edits to make it feel more familiar. Be sure it flows in the way a conversation would- contents in an order that makes sense with completed thoughts. And remember, a conversation is between two or more people so feel free to ask thought-provoking questions of the reader.

Don't worry so much about how you open the essay as you're just getting started. The first step is to just start writing. The beginning will change so many times that what you end up with likely won't hold any similarity to what you started with- this really applies to the entire piece actually. You'll slowly polish each section and blend them together as your story takes its final shape. What's really important is the lasting impression left by the essay as whole, not necessarily the beginning, end, etc.

Be open to the comments and opinions of those you allow to critique your writing but don't let their thoughts steer yours in a completely different direction that doesn't feel like your path. Again, this is about you, your opinions, your writing, your quirks, your random wonderings. Don't be tempted to let someone else's personality bleed into what is completely yours.

Formatting

Submit your essays in either Arial, Times New Roman, Cambria, or Calibri font, font size 12. If you need to highlight something, use italics, avoid bolds and underline. Use single space between lines, and hit enter twice to separate paragraphs; the Common App doesn't allow indenting.

If you're a bit of a perfectionist like myself, you may rewrite and edit your essays dozens of times before you feel good about submitting them. There's nothing wrong with that as long as you realize there is a limit to how many rewrites are actually making your essays better. There are several tools you can use to catch mistakes, but you cannot follow them blindly. Sometimes a program will suggest a change that doesn't make sense, and you will need to be discerning as to whether these changes are needed rather than just accepting all of their corrections. As you move forward into the following paragraphs, remember that grammatical errors are sometimes a practical tool when used purposefully and creatively-to make a point, to make the writing feel more personable, etc.

Personal Pronouns

Remember that whenever you refer to someone or something as *he, she, it, they, him, her, us*, or *them*, you need to establish who or what you're referencing. For example, in the sentence "I took this idea from my father; he worked in the field for many years," you know who *he* is because we establish that in the first part of the sentence. If you jump over to referencing yourself or someone else, you'll need to reestablish that *he* is referring to your father the next time you bring him up.

Comma Splices and Oxford Comma

Comma rules can be frustrating, especially because they differ depending on who you ask. A misplaced or misused comma can change the meaning of an entire sentence. One of the most common comma mistakes I see is when they're used to separate the subject from the verb. For example, "While in high school I, my good friend Michelle, along with her brother Steven, took part in several volunteer projects." Now, compare it to: "While in high school I, my good friend Michelle, along with her brother Steven took part in several volunteer projects." The author may be trying to indicate a pause with the comma after 'Steven' or was unsure whether punctuation was needed there, but it doesn't serve a grammatical purpose.

When in doubt, use the Oxford comma. It comes before the final conjunction in a list of three or more items. For example: "We are going to be wearing yellow, blue, and green suits." The Oxford comma comes after 'blue' and separates it from the last item, 'green.' Without it, there may be some confusion as to whether the suits come in three different colors or if one is yellow and one is both blue and green.

Capitalization

Use capitalization at the beginning of each sentence and to indicate proper nouns- people, places, companies, brands, and titles. If a title is made up of several words, each should be capitalized except for articles, conjunctions, and prepositions.

Should you capitalize the name of your major in your personal essay? Not necessarily. Unless the name of the major is already a proper noun or if the name comes at the beginning of a sentence, it's better not to do it. I would, however, recommend capitalizing course names.

Homophones

When two or more words are pronounced the same way but have different meanings and spellings, this is called a homophone and is very easy to overlook. Examples of homophones include:

- addition—edition
- course—coarse
- eight—ate
- troop—troupe
- weave—we've
- affect—effect

Homophones can be an issue even for the most experienced writers; even grammar software may let them slip at times. To double-check for these and any other grammatical or spelling errors, have others whose abilities you trust read the essay and point out possible areas for improvement.

Plagiarism: Seriously, Don't

No, like really, don't. Plagiarism can be damaging even if it's unintentional or isn't discovered until years later, and there are many online tools available to help you avoid it.

Plagiarism is when you use someone else's ideas and pass them off as your own without proper reference. This could mean copying text word-for-word without quotation marks or neglecting to cite your sources. Avoiding plagiarism may sound like a simple concept. All you need to do is avoid stealing other people's ideas, right? Unfortunately, people do it unintentionally all the time. Just be sure you're including proper citing to the information you're referencing.

Oftentimes, professors and admissions officers can spot plagiarism even if they haven't read the original version. They may notice when a student's writing doesn't sound natural or if the style or quality changes throughout the piece. If they feel plagiarism is afoot, they may investigate further using sophisticated software that checks through an online database of materials by authors and other students. Still, sometimes all that's needed is to Google a sentence that sounds odd to determine whether the phrase was taken verbatim from someone else's material.

Admissions officers will reject an applicant that has purposefully plagiarized. They might be flexible regarding accidental plagiarism or incorrect use of citations, but it's best not to test this. Often, the applicant has absorbed someone else's ideas over the years and doesn't realize that what they're putting on paper may not qualify as their own. This differs from transcribing the entire phrase or structure from another person's material but is still considered plagiarism.

Admissions officers will be rigorous regarding plagiarism during the application process, but this also carries over into your college years. A student caught plagiarizing may be expelled, staining their reputation and possibly affecting their chances of attending another university. Also, while it's an extreme consequence, a student guilty of plagiarism may be sued based on copyright loss and have to pay a fine to the original author.

Creating your own content isn't always easy, but it's rewarding and holds no threat of rejection or expulsion. After all, you're in college to learn and build your skills, not just to get a diploma. Challenges build character and competence.

Writing a Last-Minute Essay

Optimally you should start drafting an outline and rough draft of your essays at least a month before they are due. But many factors can delay the process. For example, maybe you're having a hard time arranging other aspects of your application, or perhaps you're just a procrastinator; nobody's perfect!

With little time to complete what could be argued as the most crucial part of your application, you may find yourself overwhelmed and panicked. The good news is that it's still possible to write an acceptable, or even a great, essay in little time. Of course, it's not the ideal way of going about it, but it's still achievable.

You cannot stretch your time, but you can use it wisely. You'll temporarily need to become an anti-procrastinator. That may mean canceling plans during this time. This could also mean sacrificing free time- weekends and whatnot for the time being. Remember, managing your time also means taking care of yourself to avoid burnout. You need to devote significant time to these efforts while still being sure to eat, sleep, and relax effectively. It's important to set realistic goals for your writing time; you are not a machine, and you'll will need some time to rest between each writing session. You could meditate, take a long shower, eat something scrumptious, or watch an episode of your favorite show, then go back to work.

With little time for preparation, start by just writing. Don't focus on grammar, spelling, or even consistency in ideas. Instead, think of this as brainstorming- answering the questions *Who am I? What are my goals? Why am I seeking further education? What am I passionate about? What are my favorite hobbies and why? Why this college?*

Among these answers, you will find the material that your essay will be built upon. If you have the option of choosing between different prompts, pick the one you're instinctively attracted to the most. Writing about what interests and excites you will make the process flow more easily.

The next step is to draft a quick outline, dividing the essay into sections in an order that makes sense. Keep in mind that you are writing about yourself for people who don't know you. Writing an essay at the last minute won't give you the chance to set it aside for a few days and come back to it, so have others review your drafts if at all possible. Get honest opinions on each essay and make minor improvements to build big impacts.

6

Eeny, Meeny, Miny, Moe

Getting that acceptance letter makes all the effort feel so worth it. You can and should celebrate it with your family and friends; it's a big accomplishment.

But after a day or two, it's time to settle down and make some decisions. This isn't over yet. The post-acceptance process can be confusing and a bit jarring at times. Stay level-headed and organized.

Take a Deep Breath and Proceed

At this point, you have a few or all of the responses from the colleges you applied to. This is the time to sit down with your family or simply those whose opinions you trust and discuss which option is right for you.

Go over your prior research and make pro/con lists for each school you've been accepted to, broken down by location, expense, class size- all the things that matter to you. Remember that you only have a certain amount of time to make your decision and respond to the universities with your decision. Unless you've been accepted to your top choice (that you've determined you can afford), allow the opportunity for all of your acceptances to come in before you make your final decision. Don't push the deadlines too much though. Eventually universities will assume you will not be attending if they don't hear back from you. Remember that it's common courtesy to reach out and inform the colleges whose offers you decline. Many students have been waitlisted and will get to hear good news from these schools that you've decided weren't right for you.

You will need to formally accept the offer through a letter, email, or their online admission system. It should read something like this:

(Date)

I, (your name), am pleased to accept your offer and look forward to joining the student body for the (year) (fall or spring) semester. You'll find all the required documents attached, including (list of documents). Thank you for the exciting opportunity.

Sincerely,

(Your name)

Pay attention to the conditions being offered with your acceptance. That goes for the program, syllabus, and any financial aid you're being offered. You don't want to accept blindly lest you risk being caught in the spiderweb of student debt you were unprepared for.

You may feel a bit bombarded with questions, requests for additional documentation, or a bunch of information being thrown at you following your acceptance including housing options and roommate agreements. Oftentimes, there are websites available to connect with other students accepted to the same school in order to find good options for roommates. Take advantage of this. I can tell you from personal experience that living with people who have similar definitions of 'clean' and 'quiet' is far more comfortable than the opposite. Once you know who your roommates will be, you can chat and get to know each other before you physically meet. Obviously, you should be prepared to share some common spaces and items, and it may be beneficial to draft some sort of agreement of your own that you're all willing to abide by.

Your university will likely set up an email account for you. You will use this account for basically all communications relevant to schooling. You'll also be given access to an organized student system, where you can get all the information you need about your courses, the goings on around campus, etc. Follow the college's social media pages, take part in various groups, and go ahead and put yourself out there in whatever ways you feel comfortable.

The Big Change

As you are dealing with all the emotion that comes along with saying goodbye to high school, there's still plenty of preparation to do. Some students will travel to another state or country; others will stay in their hometowns. It can be a sad and exciting time, but if you decide on going to college, you'll need to stay focused and be practical about the logistics of what you're going to do.

Planning is important, whether that means checking out the bus or train schedule, buying books and clothes, and of course, the dreaded budgeting. You'll also need to plan your time wisely; it's one of your most valuable assets. I recommend a great planner to maintain balance between lectures, seminars, reading, writing, new friends, and keeping yourself fed and rested. But do what works for you. You may also find it beneficial to seek part-time work. There are usually tons of positions on campus or in the general vicinity for students. Just remember that your education is your main focus; it's what you came for.

You will find that college life is much different from high school. You should expect to spend 12–16 hours in each class per week, with breaks between them. Generally, it's recommended to plan for 2-3 hours of study time on your own for each hour you spend in classes. The academic year is divided into two semesters, each with 15 weeks. The number of students in each class could vary greatly, but this will depend on the size of the university and whether the course is general education or specific to your major. Prepare to be surrounded by a dozen or a hundred fellow students.

Each professor has their own style of teaching and will expect different things from you, but they will all expect you to manage your own schedule and will assume that you're staying up to date with the material. There will be lots of independent reading and writing to be done regarding topics covered in lecture as well as additional material.

Testing may not be as frequent as you're accustomed to in high school, so they'll usually cover a lot of information. Some professors will give a brief review of what you should expect to see on upcoming exams, but others will not, so it's up to you to be sure you're reviewing everything you need to be.

The change in pace can be daunting at first. While you may spend less time in a classroom, you will have a higher workload outside of it. If you have trouble studying or completing assignments on your own, give study groups a try or work in a quiet library or study hall surrounded by other students doing the same thing. Don't be discouraged if your first few grades are not what you're accustomed to receiving in high school; this is a new challenge and will take some getting used to.

Avoiding Senioritis

So you got in.... congrats! While this is extremely exciting and should be celebrated, it doesn't mean you can lose focus on the latter half of your senior year. Senioritis is common, and it's contagious. I see it all too often, that shiny acceptance letter shows up, and motivation declines. You relax, which is excellent, but not when it's too much. The excitement of acceptance and the future can swirl into a loss of momentum and lead to a lack of effort. While some consider the term a joke due to its funny name, senioritis is a real issue that affects students every year. Classes feel like less of a challenge to conquer, and it begins to feel as though passing the course is good enough. It's okay not to feel the same enthusiasm for the syllabus as you may have once, but you don't want to undermine all the work that you've done.

Don't be too harsh on yourself- the road to senioritis is paved with stress and burnout. Dividing tasks into small chunks can make them much more manageable. Just stay organized and committed to following a schedule. Also, if possible, surround yourself with positive, encouraging people. A bad attitude can spread like wildfire.

If you're still having trouble staying focused, try changing studying spaces- your desk, the cafeteria, the library, or even the lawn. This small adjustment can do wonders for the mind. Being surrounded by different stimuli may help you approach the material with a fresh mindset.

You may be asked for an updated transcript following your conditional college acceptance so let me repeat it-don't slack on your studies leading up to graduation. It's not common for a college to withdraw an acceptance letter because the student's grades went down in the last few months of high school, but it does happen. Regardless, it's not a good look. When senioritis hits hard, take a minute to consider the value of what you're doing and how hard and long you've worked to get there. You know your story better than anyone, and you see the sacrifice it took to get to this point. Don't let that all go to waste; finish strong!

7

Dealing with the Elephant in the Room—the Bill

To be eligible for financial aid, you'll need to fill out the Free Application for Federal Student Aid (FAFSA) and renew it each year of your education. Plan on getting started in October during your senior year. Colleges use this form to award aid. Some of the eligibility requirements include being a U.S. citizen or a noncitizen with a green card and being enrolled in an eligible course of study.

You could get a private loan from a bank or credit union, but these can be expensive and generate debts that can be crippling. The U.S. government offers federal student loans, which are subjected to strict rules and offer different special benefits.

Federal student loans are tax deductible and you have the option to wait until after graduation to start repayment. With private loans, you might have to start paying while you're still at school. Federal loans also have a fixed interest rate, unlike private ones, whose interest rate could change over time.

Loans are different from grants and scholarships, requiring that you pay them back after you graduate, usually with interest. There are several repayment options, but research your options carefully as you could be making payments for several years.

Different factors carry weight in whether or not you are eligible for a grant. The size of your family, past criminal convictions, intellectual disabilities, being homeless, being in foster care, or having a parent who died during military service in Iraq or Afghanistan after 9/11 can all affect your chances of getting a grant. Once you get your grant and begin your studies, you will be assisted by the college's financial aid office, which will manage your school payments and other important costs. It's crucial that you maintain good performance during your studies, or risk losing your aid. You won't have to repay a grant after you finish your course, unless you withdraw from your courses.

Some organizations also offer scholarships as a form of investment. They are offered to students who show special talent in a certain area. There are a variety of scholarships to apply for, each of them with their own requirements. Some of them are merit-based, while others are directed at specific social groups and minorities. They may amount to a portion of your tuition or possibly even cover it entirely. The application deadline for scholarships is generally in the fall.

You can also get a work–study job, which allows you to pay for your studies through part-time work. I don't recommend planning to pay for your education with only a job held between classes. It is highly unlikely that you'll draw enough income to cover all your expenses.

The federal government also offers other forms of financial assistance for students through tax benefits and programs such as the Federal Pell Grant, the Federal Supplemental Educational Opportunity Grant (FSEOG-for those with extraordinary financial need), and the Teacher Education Assistance for College and Higher Education (TEACH) Grant (for those that firmly plan on pursuing a career in teaching). These cover not only the tuition fees but also lodgings, books, and transportation.

Applying for Aid

In order to request the documents to apply for Federal Student Aid, you will need to register for an FSA ID. Filling out the FAFSA will allow you to apply for federal grants, work-study, and loans. Once you navigate to , you'll fill out a form that includes information about your prior academic year. The FAFSA form will ask you to determine your dependency status, as well as information about your parents and their financial situation and contributions. Due to the COVID-19 pandemic, many families have experienced a sudden change in their finances. If that's true in your case, you can make that known through your FAFSA even if you've already submitted it. With your FSA ID username and password on hand, you can log into the website and submit your application. You can include up to 10 colleges on your FAFSA form, but you're still allowed to apply to other schools after you've finished your application.

To be eligible for a grant, you will need to fit certain criteria regarding the cost of the school you've been accepted to, your enrollment status, and your school record. The school should have a financial aid officer who will manage all of these aspects based on your cost of attendance (COA). The COA comprises all costs necessary for you to complete your education.

After supplying the needed information, an Expected Family Contribution (EFC) number will be generated. This is a number that financial aid officers use to calculate how much aid you'll need. The EFC is the amount of money your family is expected to contribute toward your education. That will be subtracted from your COA to determine how much more financial assistance is needed that year. Your EFC will be determined based on the taxed and untaxed income of your family. It also takes into account assets and benefits such as pensions and social security. The number of people in your family is also taken into consideration, especially if other members are also getting higher education and financial aid.

By accepting aid, you are agreeing to several rules and guidelines. It's important that you understand these rules. You should be aware of how much money you're getting, how much your family is spending, and whether you are expected to repay it after graduation.

Schools are required by federal law to offer a net price calculator (NPC) for you to estimate your COA. This cost has a ceiling, and you should be aware of what that is in case you end up not receiving any aid.

Expect your financial aid award letter from the colleges you've been accepted to by April of your senior year. This could come via email or regular post. Be sure to look for any sort of notification that your application may be missing important documents. Don't waste time in that case. Quickly provide any documents they're requesting.

Appealing for Financial Aid

One of the reasons it's important to keep your application up to date is that your financial situation can change while it's being reviewed. This may be due to loss of a job, the death of a family member, a medical emergency, or a change of address. Suddenly, the amount you requested won't serve to cover your necessities anymore.

There's always a chance that you won't get financial aid or that it's less than what you hoped for. You can appeal the decision and try again. The best way of doing that is by writing a financial aid appeal letter, in which you'll explain your situation and why you need more robust financial aid to attend college. Schools have a limited well of aid, and you need to appeal as soon as possible, before they run out of resources to offer. Contact the financial aid office through email or by phone and ask about their policy regarding the appeal process. Find out who you need to reach out to and if they have any special requirements. Be sure you are contacting the right person within the financial aid office. That's important not only for you to make sure they'll read your appeal, but also so you can address the person by their specific name, rather than something like "to whom it may concern."

Write a professional and concise email, avoiding being too flourished or using too many technical terms. Ask them to reconsider the financial aid amount, offering details as to why you need the financing. Explain your difficulties, stating whether your situation may have changed since you first applied and the difference that this aid would make in reaching your goals.

It's important to know the guidelines of appeal for each college so that you know what to include in your email. Attach any relevant documents, without overwhelming the receiver with too many files. In some cases, you will be requested to fill and attach required forms.

It helps to be specific about the amount that you need to attend school and politely show them why the amount they initially offered isn't enough. Include not only the tuition and accommodations but the specifics such as travel costs and food. Include a description of what you will be able to afford yourself with the help of your family, the part-time jobs that you might get, and other grants if that's the case.

Use the letter to detail offers you've gotten from other schools as a comparison. And, as with any professional letter, close it by thanking them for their time and for considering your appeal.

Apart from the attached documents, the entire letter really shouldn't go over one page. This may sound like a lot of information for such a short length, but keeping the letter brief and to the point will improve your chances. It's important that you write your own letter, even though you may ask others to proofread it. I'd recommend it actually as grammatical and spelling errors will detract from the strength of your writing.

An appeal might not be enough if the gap you need to fill is more than the school can help with. In that case, you'll need to consider other possibilities such as loans.

Graduate and Repay

After graduation, it'll be time to repay your student loans. Getting your degree doesn't mean you'll have your dream job with a steady income fresh out of college. With student loans, you're entitled to a grace period of six months before you have to start making payments. This is your chance to prepare and consider your repayment options. The idea is to give you time to find a job that allows you to make those loan payments. Some students actually start to make payments on their loans while still in college, reducing their debt after school. Of course, this isn't a requirement, but it's a good idea if you can.

Some repayment options for Federal college loans include:

- The standard repayment plan: A fixed amount to be paid every month with payments completed in 10 years.
- The graduated repayment plan: Payments start lower and increase every two years so that the loan is paid off in 10 years.
- The extended repayment plan: This may be a fixed or graduated payment laid out so that payments are completed in 25 years.
- The income-driven repayment plan: Payments fluctuate each year according to your conditions, generally 10% of your discretionary income. The

remaining amount can be forgiven after 20–25 years, depending on the consistency of payments.

It helps to pay more than the minimum monthly amount if you are able to. You can have your monthly payments deducted automatically from your bank account through AutoPay if you so choose. This helps to avoid incurring fees that come from missing a payment and may also offer you an interest rate deduction.

8

Deferred, Transferred, and Perturbed

After all your effort and planning, you may still find yourself as the recipient of the dreaded rejection letter. If you've been informed that you were deferred or wait-listed or that your application has been denied, you're obviously going to feel frustrated. Be careful not to overreact; all is not lost. You still have options. Be upset, be disappointed. That's normal. But then relax those shoulders, take a breath, and assess the situation.

Deferral vs Waitlist

Colleges have limited time to go through all the applications. If you applied as Early Action or Early Decision, the school may have postponed their decision on whether to admit you and will decide with the regular applicants. If you applied for regular or rolling admission, the school may need more information from you or they might wait to see your final grades and you will be deferred. They'll ask to see your updated grades or new test scores since submitting your application.

Deferrals can sometimes feel even more frustrating than being denied or waitlisted. It lengthens the entire application process in a moment when you were hoping for some closure. If the admissions officers ask you for updates, get the requested information to them as soon as possible. You might have even provided some of this material before but failed to follow certain guidelines on how to submit it. If you're given another opportunity to submit this information correctly, be sure to read and follow the instructions to the letter.

You could also find yourself on a waitlist, which means that the college finished reviewing your application and is interested in you but isn't quite sure. This is sort of a holding queue until the school is able to determine how many of the admitted students will be attending. They can't accept too few students but they certainly can't admit too many either. The waitlist creates more flexibility for the admissions office. When determining whether you're willing to wait it out for the university's decision or commit to another school, consider doing a little research on how often students are admitted from the school's waitlist and at what percentage on average. If it's a rarity that the school admits from that pool of applicants, then you may not want to take your chances.

Having several college options is helpful when you find yourself in these situations. Even being on two or more waitlists gives you a better chance of being admitted than if you've only applied to one college. Your future shouldn't depend on the decisions of one school. All that said, keep in mind that if you're deferred or waitlisted by one school but accepted by another, you should consider how the schools you've been accepted to compare to those that have put you on the waitlist or deferred you. Are you willing to deal with extending the decision process? Ultimately, it's up to you to determine whether they're worth the wait.

To appeal to a deferral or wait-listing, you need to follow the school's guidelines. If they've instructed that you don't reach out, don't. The worst thing you can do is to call or write to the admissions office and ask them to take another look at your application if they've explicitly said not to. Depending on the institution's policy, you will have an opportunity to respond to the decision, and there's always a chance you'll be accepted.

If the school welcomes such things, you have the option of emailing a letter of continued interest after being deferred or waitlisted. This lets them know that you are still interested. Students who don't write this kind of letter still have a chance of being accepted, but writing one could boost your chances. You'll use this to update the admissions officer regarding any grades, accomplishments, etc. that have changed since you submitted your application initially. Include anything relevant to your school life such as extracurricular activities and events in your personal life that could possibly influence their decision. Let them know how much you appreciate their consideration and that you're looking forward to joining them in the near future. If you were deferred or wait-listed by more than one college, the letters need to be tailored to each specific school, acknowledging that you aren't yet accepted without sounding bitter or frustrated. Don't grovel or try to invoke their sympathies. Rather, you want to inspire their acceptance with your merits.

This is also a time when your high school counselor may be able to help you form a game plan. If you have the opportunity to work with them, take full advantage and heed their advice.

Denial

While deferrals and waitlists mean that you'll have to be patient for a while longer to get a response, being denied is just what it sounds like. It's impossible not to feel disappointed when you get a rejection letter. Your application was reviewed and ultimately the AOs determined you were not quite what they were looking for. As you know by now, the college admittance process is highly competitive. Being denied a spot doesn't mean that you aren't intelligent or qualified, just that you weren't the right fit for that institution at that time. As much as it hurts, don't forget that you have other completely respectable options. Take a couple of days to digest the news, then get back to it.

Your Options After Denial

There's always a chance that you aren't accepted anywhere straightaway or you've determined that you won't be able to afford the ones that did accept you.

Taking a gap year can be a good option. Going straight from high school into college can be a disorienting experience for some, and having a year or a semester away from school will allow you to gain some life experience or work a job to save money; the possibilities are endless. You might discover new interests that will take you down a different path than you initially thought, possibly not leading to college at all.

Some people use the gap year to work or to intern in a field that relates to their desired major. Rather than making the leap from high school straight to college, some students actually prefer to take some time to get real life experience. This may even help them stand out when applying to universities later on or spark a change in their desired career path or college.

What if you decide you're just not built for academia, or vice versa? There's nothing wrong with that. Many rewarding and prestigious jobs do not require a college degree. Rest assured, you can absolutely be happy and make a good living without spending any time in a college classroom. This is not intended to discourage you from pursuing a college degree, but it's crucial to know your desires, strengths, and weaknesses before committing time and money to that pursuit.

If you're devoted to getting a degree, you can always apply to other colleges or even reapply to the ones that rejected you. Students are often offered a spot when reapplying after a denial, but there's obviously no guarantee. Your writing and resume will likely improve by the time you reapply, thereby increasing your odds of acceptance.

Learning Outside College

Education can come from many different places. Some careers require on-the-job learning and experience to succeed with no prior formal education required. Apprenticeships and internships are great opportunities to learn about all sorts of careers, from becoming a barber to getting into the stock market.

While a four-year degree may be considered prestigious, you shouldn't overlook the advantages of community college as an alternative or a preliminary to a university. These colleges offer a pleasant experience without the pressures of moving into a dorm room or a high price tag. You can complete your general education requirements there, earning a two-year Associate degree. Then you can transfer to a four-year university. In fact, this is not a bad option to plan for after high school, especially if you live near a reputable community college. Just be sure that you look into what courses/degrees will transfer to the universities you'll be applying to later. You also have the option of pursuing a course of study that will allow you to begin your career right out of community college. They offer career-specific certificates alongside academic degrees. Depending on where you attend, you can study to become a dental hygienist, medical office manager, respiratory therapist, surgical technologist, welder, or hotel manager, among many other things.

You can take courses at a community college without an SAT or ACT score, although these certainly don't hurt and can assist in making sure you're placed into the courses that are right for you. The course levels may also be determined by an ACCUPLACER test administered by the school or on your high school GPA grade. You'll likely need to provide a high school transcript or GED and a FAFSA, if you want to apply for student aid.

Community colleges are much more affordable than a four-year university. Not only is the tuition less expensive, but you won't have the same expenses with accommodations- although this will vary from student to student depending on their personal situation. Students fresh out of high school often choose to continue with their current living situation while commuting to campus or attending classes online.

Another benefit (depending on whose opinion you ask) is that class sizes at community colleges tend to be relatively small, allowing for more personalized attention from instructors.

You also have the advantage of experimenting with different types of courses to help figure out what major you want to pursue later on. So even if you're not sure at first whether to aim for a transfer to a university or if you'd like to go after a career-specific certificate, you have more room to play around a bit. Not to mention, if you start down one path and change your mind, the monetary investment is much less than it would have been at a university.

To some students, the chance of leaving home is one of the most appealing parts of going to college. But there are others who don't want to part from their hometown, their friends, and their family. Even if you're not staying at your parents' house while attending community college, you can still stay close to the people and places that matter to you.

The interactions between students and community college teachers are more similar to high school than they are with college. There's still a large amount of reading, but often the teachers can get to know many students individually rather than relying so much on a teaching assistant, or TA.

Community colleges generally offer very flexible schedules, which is extremely helpful for students who can't alter their job schedule or have family commitments but still want to further their education.

Even people who've met all the requirements to enter a four-year college might not be able to commit to the time away from home. As we've seen, the tuition fees are only the tip of the iceberg of all the costs you'll have while attending college. Some people care for children or loved ones who need assistance, but there are many responsibilities that adults need to manage. In a situation like this, going to a community college can mean the difference between being stuck in time and taking a step forward.

9

Special Circumstances

Everyone's journey into and through college looks somewhat different. But some special circumstances have slightly varying rules and guidelines- transfers, international students, athletes, homeschoolers, veterans, and students with learning disabilities, to name a few.

While each of these particular cases requires special procedures, the key aspects remain the same. That includes keeping a good profile, planning ahead, proper presentation, and writing solid essays.

Transfer Students

Being admitted to college is exciting, but somewhere down the line, you might realize it's not the right place for you or can't help you reach your goals. You'll be applying as an unplanned transfer student. Or maybe you attended community college first and are transferring to a university to pursue your Bachelor's degree. This is considered a planned transfer.

There are plenty of reasons why you could be dissatisfied with the institution you're studying at. College tuition is expensive, and if you feel that you aren't getting what you need out of the courses or campus life, there's no shame in considering other places.

Google is a great tool to determine if the college you are currently enrolled in has an articulation agreement with the one you plan to transfer to. This will outline the courses one university will accept from another. The courses may have drastically different syllabi. The transfer policies and the number of accepted transfer students vary from college to college, so contact the transfer adviser from both schools. There might be a limit to how many credits will transfer over, or they might only accept transfers at a specific time of the year. Also, this goes without saying but... keep your grades up.

Some of the principles of regular admission also apply to transfers: paying visits to the new campus, sending letters of recommendation, and scheduling interviews with the admission team, all of which demonstrate an interest in the new school.

Most colleges have either one or two application deadlines for transfer. The deadline for a fall transfer is usually around March. Spring transfer deadlines typically fall between October and December. You will probably have to access the Common App for the transfer application. Once you access the app, you'll need to offer some personal information, your academic history, and some supporting data. The same activities from your initial application apply here, but you'll provide updated info and relevant documents. Expect universities to be more interested in your community college GPA than that from high school.

Standardized test scores are sometimes requested and possibly a transfer essay. You will likely be asked to write about why you want to transfer and your goals once you've moved. Resist any urge to write or speak poorly about your current school. Veer away from drama in general when drafting your essay.

International Students

If you are an international student applying to a US college, be aware that you will have to follow specific regulations regarding financial aid, especially if it's need-based. The best way to start your research is at your local EducationUSA office or their website. You can research all about applying to and attending American colleges- information about costs and financial aid, researching your options, and applying for your student visa.

You might get a financial aid package or a merit scholarship, which covers many expenses but not all of them. Remember that you'll also need to cover flights, health insurance, and other costs of living alone in a different country.

Students that speak English as a second language are usually required to complete the Test of English as a Foreign Language (TOEFL) or the International English Language Testing System (IELTS). These tests aim to show that the student can complete the course and required reading in English.

Apart from the English test, you will have to submit a plethora of documents. If your transcript is not in English, you may be required to have it evaluated by a certified translator. Be sure the company you use to translate your documents is accepted by the university you're applying to. You should be prepared to pay somewhere between $75 and$250, and the process could take a few weeks, so don't delay.

Applying for a visa is never easy, even with assistance. To be allowed to study in the United States, you'll need an F-1 visa. After being accepted by a US college, you'll enroll with the Student and Exchange Visitor Information System (SEVIS) and be sent a form to fill out. Next, they will require you to meet with an embassy official to fill out your student visa application and interview to be sure you're eligible. I can't emphasize this enough... don't procrastinate. So much of this process takes time and can't be rushed. This visa doesn't only allow you to be able to study in the US but also allows you to work up to 20 hours a week while school is in session and up to 40 hours while school is on break.

US colleges put more weight on extracurricular activities than many other countries. But admissions officers will take into account what's available in the country you're coming from.

Getting a degree from an American college can be exciting and rewarding, but it's not always your best option. Many universities in Europe, Asia, Canada, and Africa offer valuable educational opportunities for a more affordable price. Your options are significantly increased if you are fluent in a language other than English.

Homeschooled Students

Homeschooling has become more popular over the years, with parents desiring to be more involved and have more control of their children's education and development. In addition, it's a cheaper option than a private school. It allows families to build their educational plan around their own needs and priorities rather than following the rules of a school.

Colleges are interested in good students that will contribute to academic life. Being homeschooled doesn't necessarily offer advantages or disadvantages when applying to college, but that depends on how you view it. Quality education can come in many forms, and it's a common misconception that being homeschooled automatically means you are antisocial or missed out on some major educational or social experiences. Funny enough, the exact opposite can be true. Colleges will absolutely admit homeschooled students, but they'll be held to the same standards as other applicants regarding grades, extracurriculars, community participation, etc.

The application process will be a bit different for homeschooled students. It calls for the student's legal guardian to take on the role of school counselor-assisting the student in preparations, and keeping track of transcripts and standardized test scores throughout the high school years. Responsibilities might also include letters of recommendation and providing course descriptions. Colleges will need to be provided with a school profile to give them insight into the quality of your education and explain the physical learning space. In addition, they'll need to be given your teacher's qualifications, a grading and credit system, and a report on how your schooling followed the state requirements.

This will give the admissions officers valuable context about your education. You may also be required to write extra essays or have a few more hoops to jump through than other students. Your homeschool education will need to be in accordance with your state's requirements to be able to graduate.

Homeschool curriculums may vary and offer a completely different experience from traditional schools, creating a culture shock when transitioning into college. Some students find taking a few courses at their local community college beneficial before taking the leap into a university experience. This way, they can still get college credit while allowing themselves to acclimate to the college experience.

Student-Athletes

You must be proactive if you want to apply to college as an athlete. Being talented at a sport won't get you there on its own. A coach's time is valuable, so if you want to be seen, you need to take the first step. In the middle of sophomore year, you can start to make yourself known to athletic recruiters. Start emailing college coaches, introducing yourself, and attaching videos showcasing your abilities.

The NCAA divides colleges into three divisions based on size, athletic funding, campus experience, and available athletic scholarships. Divisions I and II excel at these aspects and generally offer support to the athletes they are recruiting during the admissions process. However, division III college coaches aren't given as much influence over admissions.

Videos are the best way of getting noticed by coaches that otherwise may not get to see you play. Recording and sharing videos has never been easier, and it can reach schools anywhere in the country. Keep your video around 3–5 minutes, record it in HD, and don't worry about fancy editing or soundtrack. Be sure that the person watching the video can distinguish who you are through the number on your jersey or another distinctive feature.

Social media is another excellent tool that helps coaches to get in touch with student-athletes. Apart from your personal Facebook, Twitter, and Instagram pages, you should also have a professional page for your athletic life with pictures and videos.

You can find a copy of the "NCAA Guide for the College-Bound Student-Athlete" online. This guide lays out the rules on how college coaches can recruit athletes. Your high school might have a copy of this guide, but its rules are reassessed yearly, so make sure you have the most up-to-date version. Also, keep in mind that your performance on the court/field/etc. is only one of many factors that will influence your athletic application.

As an athlete, you need to consider if you'll be able to divide your time between playing sports and your studies. Is your goal to play professionally, or are you using sports as a tool to get an education? Together with the school counselor, your high school coaches could be of great help in building your college list. The athletic recruiting process is long, and it's best to begin as early as possible.

Campus visits will help you get a feel for the place, including how sports are handled in general. Try to watch at least one game, observe a practice or training session, get to know the facilities, and talk to the coach.

Focus on your visits to schools that have already shown an interest in you, and do the proper research so you can have a productive conversation with the coaches. The fact that a coach wants you on the team doesn't mean you're automatically accepted into that college. Still, depending on the school, this can be a significant factor.

Veteran Students

Veterans often desire to go back to school and complete their education after finishing their service. One of the reasons many young men and women enter the military is so that their education will be paid for after a certain number of years of service. Thankfully, they can count on assistance from the government to fulfill that dream, and rightfully so.

Over two million military service members have received assistance to get an education through the Post-9/11 GI Bill. These benefits can even be transferred to their families, as long as they remain active in the armed forces. They cover in-state school tuition fees, as well as costs associated with private and foreign schools up to $17,500 annually, including expenses to take admission tests.

Veterans are eligible for the program for 36 months, extending to 48 if they enroll in more than one program. If you fit into this group, you should start by learning all you can about the benefits you're entitled to. The US Department of Veterans Affairs Education telephone line (1-888-442-4551) is there to help you work through any questions you might have. It can be hard to adapt to civilian life after experience in the service, and academic life is no exception.

It's possible to get college credit through the military, especially if you are pursuing a degree based on matters related to your training. You can also provide valuable contributions to the course through your personal experience.

Students With Learning Differences

Students with learning differences encompass those with learning gaps such as dyslexia, dyscalculia, dysgraphia, and attention deficit hyperactivity disorder. These students may require special conditions or accommodations to complete their courses.

Letting colleges know that you have a learning difference won't harm your applications. While schools don't have a quota of students with disabilities that they are required to admit, they generally value diversity.

The Individualized Education Plan (IEP), which guarantees rights to students with disabilities, is terminated upon high school graduation. Colleges work under Section 504, which ensures they will provide accommodations to students with disabilities, as long as it doesn't change the basic nature of the program. Some students with disabilities only need unique accommodation, while others also require specialized instruction. The 504 Plan needs to be updated every year to prove that the student is being provided with what's needed. For example, a student who needs a wheelchair to get around can still take the course under normal academic conditions. A student who's hearing impaired might need the aid of a sign language interpreter. Someone with dyslexia might find it easier to type on a tablet rather than writing information down with a pen.

A student with learning differences still needs to apply through regular means. When submitting your application, you should make the school aware of what kind of disability you have, even if you don't feel you'll need special treatment. Don't assume that this will give you an advantage over other students, but it can fill in gaps in your transcript.

As we've discussed, applying to a college isn't only about finding out if you're right for them but also if they're right for you. This is even more important when it comes to students with disabilities. They'll need to make sure the schools they're applying to will be able to provide conditions that are conducive to completing their education.

Campus visits are a great way of checking out how the college deals with different types of student disabilities. You can also learn about what accommodations they offer through their website. Take this research process seriously, as this could affect how simple or difficult it is to go about your daily campus life.

It's crucial that students with learning differences can self-advocate for what they need during their academic years. Every day is going to be a challenge, and you need to be able to speak up when you don't have what you need to go about your studies unless you can provide these things for yourself. For example, a student who uses a wheelchair and needs an elevator to access the library can't conform to that elevator being out of service for several days. This is the type of situation when you'll need to ask for help. You aren't and shouldn't be expected to do everything on your own, just as any student shouldn't.

10

Conclusion

Not everyone is built for academia. That doesn't mean they are not gifted, intelligent, or resourceful. Everyone has their own talents and strengths, which don't always match up with the requirements of the college world.

Most people enter college to start a career. Some may choose to major in business as they planned for years, while others may decide to abandon their initial plan and follow an academic career through teaching and research. Still, some students will decide that this isn't what they are looking for. The effort and money they're putting into their higher education aren't going to pay off in the way they hoped, or they don't actually want to pursue the career they initially thought.

You will have to take the lead regarding your applications, although you will hopefully have support from those around you. You'll spend a lot of time researching schools, studying for exams, and scheduling interviews, among everything else. This isn't something that you can do on autopilot. All this effort requires passion and dedication that doesn't come out of thin air.

The process of getting accepted into college is indeed an art, with a bit of science thrown in. Scientists study what was done before them and work to improve and perfect that knowledge. An artist taps into creativity and finds their own path. But they also study theory and familiarize themselves with the work of those who came before them. Just as no two artists are the same, each person who aspires for a college education will have a different story to tell about their struggles, triumphs, and lessons learned.

Just as a painter knows what to mix to produce the colors they want, you now have a thorough knowledge of the path ahead. Some parts of this book have likely been discouraging and others uplifting. Remember the introduction story of the egg, the coffee bean, and the carrot and what happens when they're added to boiling water. The egg gets tougher, the coffee alters its surroundings, and the carrot becomes softer. If that story didn't make much sense to you earlier, I hope it does now.

Being tough doesn't mean always being right or forcing your ideas on others. It's about believing in your skills and the idea that you will emerge from any situation wiser and stronger. It means learning how to fall rather than never falling so that the next time you hit the ground, it doesn't hurt as much.

Changing your surroundings doesn't mean forcing others to conform or training them to think like you per se. It has more to do with your capacity to influence those around you positively. The coffee bean personality knows they have a lot to share and is open to dialogue, making things a little bit better for everyone.

The carrot personality is afraid of change, which tends to weaken them. This would be the student who gives up studying a new subject because they didn't understand it at first. They schedule interviews but don't show up; they are too intimidated to try. They're afraid to include their dream college in the prospect list because they've already convinced themselves they won't be accepted.

It might sound silly, but the good news is that you don't have to be a carrot if you don't want to. I wrote this book for all students who wish to take a shot at college life. My goal was to demystify the confusion surrounding college applications and show everyone—including carrots—what they are capable of with little effort.

Anyone who sets their mind on what they want can accomplish incredible things. But having instructions about how to reach your goals will put you ahead of the game. As you arrive at these last pages, I hope you have at least a bit more knowledge than when you began reading. It's time to put it to use!

As I said in the introduction, I hope this book will be a companion to guide you through the academic side of what I'd consider to be some of the most trying years of your life. Take it with you to campus and put it on your bookshelf for reference.

You've taken a significant step toward your college goals by reading this book. Everything that happens now—the preparation, the application, the campus visits, all the way to getting accepted and starting your academic life—will represent new and challenging steps for you. New experiences will build you up, and I hope they will help you develop resilience as you go through your adult life.

If you enjoyed the book, please leave a review on Amazon. Reviews help other students like yourself to find the resources they need. I aim to make this kind of knowledge accessible; not every student can pay for professional help to guide them through this process. You never know, one of these students might schedule a campus visit soon, and you'll be the one to greet them and show them around.

11

Glossary

Accuplacer Test: A test that evaluates students' reading, writing, and math skills. It's comprised of a series of multiple-choice questions and a writing test.

Admission Rate: The percentage rate of new students a college accepts compared to how many apply each year.

Admission Requirements: The guidelines that must be followed by students who want to have their application considered. These go from providing transcripts to paying an application fee.

Admission Tests: A standardized test through which a college can evaluate each student's preparedness level. The most common ones are the ACT and the SAT.

American College Testing (ACT): Standard college admission test recognized by most colleges. It consists of five sections (English, math, reading, science, and an optional essay) with scores ranging from 1 to 36.

Application Fee: A fee that students must pay to have their submissions considered. Usually between $25 and $100.

College Application Essay: A piece of written work that a student must write and submit together with their grades and transcripts. The essay is one of the main pillars of the college application and has a substantial impact on the admissions officer's final decision.

College Board: A nonprofit organization that administers the most important standardized tests for prospective college students.

College Credit: A recognition of how much a student applied themselves to a course. Often earned through testing such as AP Exams.

Common App: An app that allows students to send applications to over 900 colleges on different continents.

Community College: Affordable institutions that provide a two-year education that can lead to a four-year degree.

Cost of Attendance (COA): The total amount of money it will cost a student to complete their studies.

Demonstrated Interest (DI): A way for student to let admissions officers know that they're serious about their academic life. That interest may be shown through actions and words.

Early Action (EA): A special deadline that gets a response before the regular decision date. It's more flexible than early decision, and students can choose to decline the offer if it doesn't suit them.

Early Decision (ED): This also allows for an earlier response, but by applying for early decision, a student is bound to attend the university they've been accepted to. If selected for early decision, they must retract their submissions to any other colleges they've applied to.

Elective: Activities that aren't a part of a chosen major but offer college credit.

Expected Family Contribution (EFC): The expected financial contribution from the student's family toward their college education.

Financial Aid: This includes all types of assistance to help pay for courses- grants, scholarships, loans, etc.

Gap Year: A period in which a student takes a break between high school and college to pursue other interests.

Grade Point Average: The calculation of a student's average performance through their grade results.

Grace Period: A period of six months following graduation, after which the student has to start paying back their federal loans.

Grants: Grants can come from the government, nonprofit organizations, or the college itself. Unlike loans, you don't have to repay them later on.

Ivy League: An association of the oldest and most prestigious colleges in America.

Letters of Recommendation: A formal letter, usually written by a teacher or school employee, to be read by admissions officers. Generally used to convince AO's to admit the student into their college.

Loan: Financial aid that has to be repaid.

Major: The main area of expertise that a student studies in college.

SAT: Together with the ACT, the most common standardized test to evaluate if a student is ready for college. Scores range from 400 to 1,600.

Scholarship: A way of financing studies through academic and other types of excellence. Scholarships are merit-based, and a high-quality performance must be maintained to keep it.

Transcript: The record of a student's school life, including grades, class attendance, discipline, and anything that will help the college admissions officers decide whether to offer a spot.

Undergraduate: A college student that hasn't yet received their Bachelor's or equivalent degree.

Veteran Students: Students who served in the armed forces

12

References

ACT. (n.d.). *Things to do after receiving a college acceptance letter.* https://www.act.org/content/act/en/students-and-parents/college-planning-resources/college-and-career-planning/what-to-do-after-receiving-acceptance-letter.html

Adler, M. H. (2020, November 17). *Essential advice for hiring an independent college advisor.* CollegeXpress. https://www.collegexpress.com/counselors-and-parents/parents/articles/high-school-journey/essential-advice-hiring-independent-college-advisor/

Alcantara, J. (2008, April). *You will never see me fall.* Family Friend Poems. https://www.familyfriendpoems.com/poem/you-will-never-see-me-fall

Applying to college as a student athlete. (n.d.). The Princeton Review. https://www.princetonreview.com/college-advice/student-athletes

ASO Staff Writers. (2022, May 26). *Choosing the right college when you've been accepted to several.* Accredited Schools Online. https://www.accreditedschoolsonline.org/resources/choose-between-colleges-after-acceptance/

Belasco, A. (2021a, January 18). *How to apply to a US college as an international student.* College Transitions. https://www.collegetransitions.com/blog/how-to-apply-to-a-us-college-as-an-international-student/

Belasco, A. (2021b, November 4). *Transfer applicants: How to complete the Common Application.* College Transitions. https://www.collegetransitions.com/blog/transfer-applicants-how-to-complete-the-common-application/

Bergman, D. (2017a, November 26). *Getting into college with a learning disability/ADHD.* College Transitions. https://www.collegetransitions.com/blog/navigating-college-with-a-learning-disability/

Bergman, D. (2021b, November 19). *How should 9th graders prepare for college?* College Transitions. https://www.collegetransitions.com/blog/how-should-9th-graders-prepare-for-college/

Berkman, J. (2020, January 27). *The 14 college interview questions you must prepare for.* PrepScholar. https://blog.prepscholar.com/college-interview-questions-you-should-prepare-for

Booth, J. (2020, November 6). *5 solid backup plans for when you don't get accepted anywhere.* College Covered. https://www.collegecovered.com/getting-into-college/

5-solid-backup-plans-for-when-you-dont-get-accepted-anywhere/

Calcagnini, L. (2016, July 23). *Where to begin? 6 personal essay brainstorming exercises*. CollegeVine Blog. https://blog.collegevine.com/where-to-begin-3-personal-essay-brainstorming-exercises/

Carignan, N. (2022, June 1). *Reasons to attend a community college vs. university*. Mount Wachusett Community College. https://mwcc.edu/blog/reasons-to-attend-a-community-college-vs-university/

College Board. (2022, January 20). *How to pick AP courses*. https://blog.collegeboard.org/how-pick-ap-courses

College Board. (March 8, 2022). *3 reasons to take AP exams*. https://blog.collegeboard.org/3-reasons-take-ap-exams

Clodfelter, K. (2022, January 26). *5 questions admissions officers want applicants to ask*. College Covered. https://www.collegecovered.com/getting-into-college/questions-to-ask-college-admissions-officers/

CollegeVine College Essay Team. (2015, December 6). *How to write a last minute essay*. CollegeVine Blog. https://blog.collegevine.com/how-to-write-a-last-minute-essay/

CollegeVine College Essay Team. (2020, July 1). *The diversity college essay: How to write a stellar essay*. CollegeVine Blog. https://blog.collegevine.com/4-tips-for-writing-a-diversity-college-essay/

College interview tips. (n.d.). My Future. https://myfuture.com/college/college-interview-tips

College planning timeline. (n.d.). My Future. https://myfuture.com/college/college-planning-timeline

Desai, P. (2021, January 20). *SAT subject tests + essay discontinued: How this impacts college admissions*. CollegeVine Blog. https://blog.collegevine.com/major-sat-changes-2021/

Dix, W. (2018, April 23). *Six ways to work with your college counselor*. Forbes. https://www.forbes.com/sites/willarddix/2018/04/23/six-ways-to-work-with-your-college-counselor/?sh=74b24cbc8cfa

Done with applications? now set your facebook to private. (n.d.). College Essay Guy. https://www.collegeessayguy.com/blog/set-facebook-to-private-after-applying

Eight Common College Essay Mistakes. (2021, April 7). Private Prep. https://privateprep.com/blog/eight-common-college-essay-mistakes/

Elkjer, B. (2021, July 8). *How to end your college essay: 5 strategies*. CollegeVine Blog. https://blog.collegevine.com/how-to-end-your-college-essay/

Essential tips for veterans applying to college. (n.d.). College Essay Guy. https://www.collegeessayguy.com/blog/veterans-college-application

Fang, L. (2020, July 8). *5 awesome college essay topics + sample essays*. CollegeVine Blog.

https://blog.collegevine.com/good-college-essay-topics/

Federal Student Aid. (n.d.a). *11th grade college prep checklist.* https://studentaid.gov/resources/prepare-for-college/checklists/11th-grade

Federal Student Aid. (n.d.b). *Federal versus private loans.* https://studentaid.gov/understand-aid/types/loans/federal-vs-private

Federal Student Aid. (n.d.c). *How financial aid works.* https://studentaid.gov/h/understand-aid/how-aid-works

Federal Student Aid. (n.d.d). *How to renew your FAFSA® application.* https://studentaid.gov/apply-for-aid/fafsa/renew

Federal Student Aid. (n.d.e). *9th grade college prep checklists.* https://studentaid.gov/resources/prepare-for-college/checklists/9th-grade

Federal Student Aid. (n.d.f). *10th grade college prep checklists.* https://studentaid.gov/resources/prepare-for-college/checklists/10th-grade

Federal Student Aid. (n.d.g). *12th grade college prep checklists.* https://studentaid.gov/resources/prepare-for-college/checklists/12th-grade

Federal Student Aid. (n.d.h). *Who gets aid.* https://studentaid.gov/understand-aid/eligibility

Federal Student Aid. (n.d.i). *Wondering how the amount of your federal student aid is determined?*

https://studentaid.gov/complete-aid-process/how-calculated

5 things homeschooled students need on their college application. (2019, October 22). Weadmit. https://www.weadmit.com/blog/5-things-homeschooled-students-need-on-their-college-application

George, T. (2022, May 19). *How to avoid plagiarism*. Scribbr. https://www.scribbr.com/plagiarism/how-to-avoid-plagiarism/

Grammar Here. (2020, March 22). *100 examples of homophones*. English Grammar Here. https://englishgrammarhere.com/vocabulary/100-examples-of-homophones/

Gunter, E. B. (2021, December 2). *College admissions glossary: Terms you need to know*. KD College Prep. https://kdcollegeprep.com/college-admissions-glossary/

Hamblet, E. (2022, March 23). *Myths about college admissions and students with learning disabilities and ADHD*. LD Advisory. https://ldadvisory.com/myths-about-college-admissions/

Helhoski, A. (n.d.). *How to write a financial aid appeal letter*. NerdWallet. https://www.nerdwallet.com/article/loans/student-loans/financial-aid-appeal-letter

Hogarth, T. (n.d.a.). *4 grammar mistakes that could kill your college essay*. College Essay Advisors: Admissions Essay Experts. https://www.collegeessayadvisors.com/grammar-mistakes-that-could-kill-your-college-essay/

Hogarth, Thea. (n.d.b.). *3 easy steps for writing a last-minute college essay.* College Essay Advisors: Admissions Essay Experts. https://www.collegeessayadvisors.com/last-minute-college-essay-early-deadline/

How to balance high school and a part-time job. (2021, December 13). eCampusTours. https://www.ecampustours.com/for-students/career-exploration/building-your-resume/how-to-balance-high-school-and-a-part-time-job.aspx#.YmWON9rMLIW

How to combine your college essay prompts. (n.d.). College Essay Guy. https://www.collegeessayguy.com/blog/college-essay-prompts

How to write a great letter of continued interest. (n.d.). College Essay Guy. https://www.collegeessayguy.com/blog/letter-of-continued-interest

How to write the community essay: Complete guide + examples. (n.d.). College Essay Guy. https://www.collegeessayguy.com/blog/community-essay

How to write the "why this major" college essay. (n.d.). College Essay Guy. https://www.collegeessayguy.com/blog/why-major-college-essay

Igoe, K. J. (2018, May 17). *Essential grammar rules for your college apps*. CollegeVine Blog. https://blog.collegevine.com/essential-grammar-rules-for-your-college-apps/

International Baccalaureate. (n.d.). *Why IB is different*. https://www.ibo.org/benefits/why-the-ib-is-different/

Joyce University. (2022, April 26). *The most common writing mistakes on college essays*. https://www.joyce.edu/blog/common-writing-mistakes-avoid/

King's College. (n.d.). *How is college different from high school?* https://www.kings.edu/admissions/hs_sophomores_and_juniors/preparing_for_college/high_school_vs_college

Last minute college application essay tips. (2021, December 17). Essay Coaching. https://www.essaycoaching.com/last-minute-college-application-essay-tips

Lopez, A. (2015, December 13). *How to use rhetorical devices in your college essay*. CollegeVine Blog. https://blog.collegevine.com/how-to-use-rhetorical-devices-in-your-college-essay/

Mathur, S. (2018a, February 10). *9 rules for requesting letters of recommendation from teachers*. CollegeVine Blog. https://blog.collegevine.com/9-rules-for-requesting-letters-of-recommendation-from-teachers/

Mathur, S. (2018b, February 20). *High school extracurriculars to join & how to prioritize them*. CollegeVine Blog. https://blog.collegevine.com/how-to-prioritize-your-high-school-extracurriculars

MBA Crystal Ball. (2019, March 22). *College admission essay plagiarism: How do professors know if you copied essays?* https://www.mbacrystalball.com/college-admission-essay-plagiarism/

Milliman, H. (2019, January 20). 3 *tips for writing a successful letter of continued interest*. PrepScholar. https://blog.prepscholar.com/letter-of-continued-interest-sample

Mitchell, T., & Moody, J. (2019, October 21). *9 things prospective college transfer students need to know*. U.S. News & World Report. https://www.usnews.com/education/best-colleges/slideshows/10-things-prospective-college-transfer-students-need-to-know

Moody, J. (2020, June 10). *What a gap year is and how it prepares students for college*. U.S. News & World Report. https://www.usnews.com/education/best-colleges/articles/2019-03-08/what-a-gap-year-is-and-how-it-prepares-students-for-college

O'Shaughnessy, L. (2011, June 14). *Learning disabilities can offer college admission edge*. U.S. News & World Report. https://www.usnews.com/education/blogs/the-college-solution/2011/06/14/learning-disabilities-can-offer-college-admission-edge

Powell, F. (2018, July 18). *How home schooling affects college admissions*. U.S. News & World Report. https://www.usnews.com/education/best-colleges/articles/2018-07-18/how-home-schooling-affects-college-admissions

Richardson, A. (2016, April 25). *17 test taking tips for mindblowing results*. Smart Student Secrets. https://www.smartstudentsecrets.com/testtakingtipsformindblowingresults/

Schine, L. B. (2018, September 10). *11 tips for proofreading and editing your college essay*. CollegeVine Blog. https://blog.collegevine.com/11-tips-for-proofreading-and-editing-your-college-essay/

Schritter, T. (2021, May 7). *What does it mean to be waitlisted or deferred?* Colleges of Distinction. https://collegesofdistinction.com/advice/what-does-it-mean-to-be-waitlisted-or-deferred/

7 tips for how to pay off student loans. (2020, July 16). CollegeData. https://www.collegedata.com/resources/money-matters/7-tips-for-how-to-pay-off-student-loans

6 things to know about demonstrated interest (from a former admissions counselor). (n.d.). College Essay Guy. https://www.collegeessayguy.com/blog/demonstrated-interest

Testing Tips. (n.d.). My Future. https://myfuture.com/college/testing-tips

The George Washington University. (n.d.). *Transitioning from high school to college: A spotlight on Section 504*. https://www.heath.gwu.edu/transitioning-high-school-college-spotlight-section-504#:%7E:text=Under%20Section%20504%2C%20colleges%20are

The homeschooler's guide to getting into college. OnlineCollege.org. (2013, August 22). https://www.onlinecollege.org/2012/06/11/the-homeschoolers-guide-to-getting-into-college/

Thompson, J. (2022, February 24). *Don't let these FAFSA mistakes cost you money*. College Covered.

https://www.collegecovered.com/paying-for-college/common-fafsa-mistakes/

3 types of federal financial aid | learn what they are. (n.d.). Citizens Bank. https://www.citizensbank.com/learning/types-of-federal-financial-aid.aspx

Tips for applying to college as a homeschooler. (n.d.). College Essay Guy. https://www.collegeessayguy.com/blog/applying-to-college-homeschooler

Tips for students with learning differences when applying to college. (n.d.). College Essay Guy. https://www.collegeessayguy.com/blog/learning-difference-college-application

University of Portland. (n.d.). *College entrance exams - What admissions tests to take and how to prepare*. https://www.up.edu/ready-for-college/college-entrance-exams-tests.html

Vaiana, D. (2020, December 22). *How different are college and high school? (Hint: Very)*. College Info Geek. https://collegeinfogeek.com/college-vs-high-school/

Wallis, A. (2018, October 31). *What is Senioritis and is There a Cure?* Southern New Hampshire University. https://www.snhu.edu/about-us/newsroom/education/what-is-senioritis

Weheba, F. (2020, January 11). *Prepare for your alumni interview*. Empowerly. https://empowerly.com/blog/prepare-for-your-alumni-interview

What is the difference between an IEP and a 504 plan? | AccessComputing. (n.d.). https://www.washington.edu/accesscomputing/what-dif

ference-between-iep-and-504-plan#:%7E:text=The%20Individualized%20Educational%20Plan%20(IEP

What to do if you've been deferred, denied, or accepted. (2019, March 21). Private Prep. https://privateprep.com/blog/deferred-denied-or-accepted/

Why this college essay guide + examples. (n.d.). College Essay Guy. https://www.collegeessayguy.com/blog/why-this-college-essay

Wickline, V. (2018, November 23). *Creating the first draft of your college application essay.* CollegeVine Blog. https://blog.collegevine.com/creating-the-first-draft-of-your-college-application-essay/

Writing a college essay. (n.d.d). My Future. https://myfuture.com/college/writing-a-college-essay

Your college admissions essay: Six ways to create a memorable closing. (2012, September 19). College Essay Solutions. https://collegeessaysolutions.com/your-college-admissions-essay-six-ways-to-create-a-memorable-closing/

Your top GI bill questions answered. (n.d.). U.S. Veterans Magazine. https://usveteransmagazine.com/2022/02/top-gi-bill-questions-answered/

You've decided! What's next? (2020, November 18). CollegeData. https://www.collegedata.com/resources/prepare-and-apply/youve-decided-on-a-college.-whats-next

Made in the USA
Monee, IL
06 March 2023